BASIL CHR. PETRACOS
CURATOR OF THE MUSEUM AT DELPHI

DELPHI

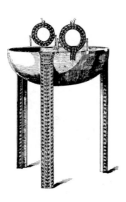

ATHENS
«ESPEROS» EDITION

The cover design is a representation on a white kylix found in the area of the Museum at Delphi (inv. No 8140). In an atmosphere of absolute serenity, Apollo, divinely beautiful, sitting on a d i p h r o s makes a libation from the phiale he is holding in his right hand, as a priest, while in his left hand he is holding the lyre. On the left, one of the wild pigeons that used to flock around the sanctuary of Apollo in antiquity.

The kylix dates from the third decade of the 5th c. B. C., i.e. from the same period as the «Charioteer». The painter — one of the greatest of antiquity according to the artistic value of his work — is unknown.

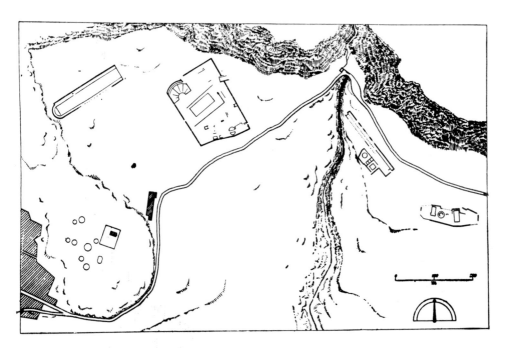

General topographical plan of Delphi (P. de La Coste-Messelière).

INTRODUCTION

The Site of Delphi: Delphi form a part of Phocis (altitude approx. 570 m.) and occupied in antiquity an important geographical position, being situated at a crossroads. The road leading from northeastern and eastern Greece to the plain of Amfissa, where it met the road joining northern Greece with Naupactus, passed through Delphi. From the beach of Itea, again, it was easy to cross to nearby Peloponnesus.

The town of Delphi and its shrines lay at the foot of two enormous crags of Mt. Parnassus —the Phedriads— *Yambia* on right and *Nauplia* on the left (though there is some uncertainty as to the latter name). Today, they are known as *Fleboukos* and *Rhodhini*, respectively. It is these crags that lend the Delphic landscape its singular and incomparable beauty. Opposite, the lengthy Mt. of Desphina (*Kirphys*) blocks the horizon and in-between lies a valley overgrown with olivetrees and traversed by a river, the *Pleistos*. The olive groves of Chrisso and Amfissa, like a sea of trees, extend down to the Itea Bay with its azure water sparkling in the sunlight. This is the famous *Krissaean Plain*, dedicated to Apollo in antiquity. Its ownership was often disputed and often brought disaster to such as would deprive the god of his own by attempting to take advantage of its fertile soil.

The History of Delphi: Information about the earliest periods of the history of Delphi has been obtained by archaeological research. From the excavations carried out in the area,

3

we know that in the period now called «Mycenaean» (14th to 11th c. B.C.), Delphi was a small village whose inhabitants worshipped a female deity, the original owner of the place, goddess Earth. Clay figurines of this deity were found in the deepest layers of the sanctuaries of Apollo and Athena Pronaie (see p. 26 and 44).

Later, during the «Geometric» period (11th to 9th c. B.C.), the sanctuary of goddess Earth was taken over by Apollo. The change is seen in the ex-votoes offered to the deity: bronze male figurines now replace the female clay statuettes.

As time passed, Delphi grew and the sanctuary of Apollo assumed a more definite shape. Excavations brought to light the remains of precincts that grew ever wider, enclosing increasingly larger spaces. The 6th c. B.C. marks the completion of the sanctuary of Apollo and the height of its material prosperity and spiritual ascendancy.

In the history of Delphi, at least up to the 4th c. B.C., the *Amphictyonia* played the leading role, protecting the site against the expansionist tendencies of the Phocians, who surrounded it. The Amphictyonia was a union of neighbouring towns pursuing common political aims. From the 7th c. onwards, the Amphictyonia was in fact an alliance of the tribes of central Greece and Thessaly, centred at the sanctuary of Demeter at Anthele near *Pylae* or *Thermopylae*; it was dominated by the Thessalians and Delphi was a member. The Amphictyonia gradually became a decisive factor in the administration of the sanctuary of Apollo and, naturally, influenced its attitudes, in political matters especially. Each member - state sent two delegates to the Amphictyonia, known as *pylagoras* and *hieromnemon*, respectively, the latter exercising the right of vote at the meetings, which were held twice annually: at Delphi in the spring and at Pylae (Thermopylae) in the autumn.

In the early 6th c. B.C., Delphi became for the first time involved in historical events. The powerful nearby city of Krissa, ancient metropolis of Delphi situated in the approximate location of the present village of Chrisso, tried to profit from the traffic gravitating to the shrine of Apollo and from the wealth flowing into Delphi. Since it could have no part in the administration of the oracle and the handling of its finances, it imposed a levy on pilgrims and official city delegates and envoys coming to the sanctuary. This created a mounting tension in the relations of Delphi and the Amphictyonia to Krissa, finally leading to war, in which Krissa was defeated (First Sacred War, 600-590 B.C.). The confirmation of Delphi's independence resulted in improved organisation of the sanctuary of Apollo. The *Pythian Games,* held in commemoration of Apollo's victory over Python, were thoroughly reorganised by the Amphictyonia and celebrated every four years. The ritual observed at the oracle assumed definite shape which remained unchanged from the time of Croesus to the time of Hadrian.

In 548 B.C., the temple of Apollo was destroyed by fire and rebuilt in the following years by contributions from Greek and foreign sponsors (see p. 20) ; the extensive construction work undertaken at the same time within the sacred precinct accounts for the main features of the sanctuary visible at the present time.

During the Persian Wars, the sanctuary adopted a rather unexpected attitude. From fear of being destroyed by the Asian invaders, it gave oracular responses that caused terror and disappointment to the Greeks. The Persians did attack it, nevertheless; but rain and bolts of lightning and rocks falling from the Phedriads drove them to flight. To commemorate this event, the Delphians erected a trophy at the shrine of Athene Pronaia (see p. 28).

In 448 B.C., the Phocians occupied Delphi, were driven away by the Lacedemonians, who marched against them (Second Sacred War) and recaptured it with the help of the Athenians. The sanctuary was not to regain its old independence until 421 B.C.

In 373 B.C., an earthquake caused the fall of large boulders from the Phedriads destroying the temple of Apollo which had been built by the Alcmeonidae. Delphi again appealed for foreign help and by 330 B.C. a new temple had been built.

In 356 B.C., the Third Sacred War started. The immediate cause was the heavy tax imposed by the Amphictyonians upon the Phocians as a punishment for having cultivated some fields belonging to the sanctuary. Athenians and Lacedemonians now formed an alliance to support the Phocians, thus hoping to put a stop to the interference of Philip of Macedonia in the affairs of southern Greece and the sanctuary, and to check «Macedonian imperialism».

The Phocians under Philomelus captured Delphi, fortified it and held it until 346 B.C. During this occupation, the Phocians, hard pressed to meet the expenses of the war, stripped the shrines of Apollo and Athene from their precious offerings including the tripod of Plataea and the shield dedicated to Athene by king Croesus (see p. 28). But the intervention of Philip of Macedonia in 346 B.C. resulted in the defeat of the Phocians who were forced to pay a large sum in compensation for the damage they had caused; the Phocians also lost their votes at the Amphictionic Council to Philip.

In 339 B.C., the Fourth Sacred War broke out against the Locrians of Amfissa who had trespassed upon the plain of Krissa which was dedicated to Apollo. Once again Philip interfered —this time as against of the Amphictyonic Council — vanquished the sacrilegious Krissans, destroyed their town and them, proceeding to Chaeronea, defeated in 338 B.C. the combined forces of Athens and Sparta who had allied against him. From this time on the Macedonians became a determining influence in Greek affairs.

Work at the construction of the new temple had continued on and off throughout the Third and Fourth Sacred Wars and by 330 B.C. it was completed and solemnly inaugurated.

In 279 B.C., the Gauls under Vrennus attacked Delphi with the intention to seize its treasures, but the Aetolians, now masters of Delphi, succeeded in routing the barbarians with the help of Apollo who — as legend has it — sent rain, snow and rocks flying upon their heads. To commemorate this great victory, the Aetolians instituted a new yearly festival comparable to the Pythian Games: the *Soterian Games* in honour of Zeus Soter (Saviour) and Apollo.

In 191 B.C., the control of the oracle passed from the Aetolians to the Romans; and from then on, especially after Roman power was consolidated by the victory of the Roman general Aemilius Paulus over the Macedonian king Perseus at Pydna in 168 B.C., Delphi obeyed the orders of Rome. The sanctuary ceased exercising any political activity or attempting to influence political affairs by its oracular responses.

In 86 B.C., the Roman General Sylla, at a loss for resources to finance the siege of Athens removed from the shrine of Apollo whatever precious metal offerings were left, including a silver jar dedicated by Croesus.

In 83 B.C., Delphi was raided and pillaged by the Thracian Maedi. It is reported that the sacred fire which had been burning in the temple for centuries was extinguished on that occasion and that the temple itself was damaged. But the sanctuary had already practically ceased to exist. The Roman emperors partly tried to support it and partly contributed to its downfall. In 67 A.D., Nero visited Delphi, took part in the Pythian Games and shipped to Rome some 500 statues from the shrine of Apollo; he also gave to his soldiers the plain of Krissa — the cause of so many wars. In 84 A.D., Emperor Domitian had some minor repairs done to the temple, and immortalised his contribution by the huge Latin inscription now kept at the Museum.

Emperor Hadrian visited Delphi twice (in 125 and in 129 A.D.) and expressed his favour in many different ways; he provided funds for the restoration of buildings and attempted to revive the Amphictyonia, an institution that had become entirely meaningless. Priest of Apollo during that period was Hadrian's friend and famous writer Plutarch of Chaeronea, who dedicated some of his dialogues to Delphic subjects (*The Obsolescence of Oracles, The E at Delphi, The Oracles at Delphi no longer given in verse*); these dialogues are invaluable sources of every kind of information about the sanctuary of Apollo.

Also in Hadrian's time, Herodes Atticus spent enormous amounts of money to equip the Delphic stadium with stone seats (see p. 24). But none of these efforts could avail any more, since Delphi was dead having lost its spiritual meaning. People no longer believed in Apollo; they were turning in ever increasing numbers to the faith of Christ.

Constantine the Great, after having attended ceremonies in his honour at Delphi, removed works of art from the sanctuary to adorn his new capital, Constantinople. Of these, only the three bronze snakes from the tripod of Plataea have been preserved (see p. 18). Emperor Julian (360–363 A.D.), later known as the Apostate, attempted to revive the ancient religion. Literary tradition has preserved an oracle supposedly given by the Pythia to the physician Oreibasius, Julian's envoy to Delphi:

> *Tell the King, the fairwrought hall has fallen to the ground,*
> *no longer has Phoebus a hut, nor a prophetic laurel,*
> *nor a spring that speaks. The water of speech even is quenched.*

Authentic or not, the oracle expresses an unquestionable truth: the death of Apollo's cult and the downfall of his sanctuary.

The Legend and the God: The original cause of the establishment of an oracle at Delphi was the existence of a «gap» in the earth giving forth vapours which had a purifying effect on animals and humans. People purified by the inhalation of these vapours became clairvoyant and predicted the future. Because of this gap, a primitive oracle was first established, dedicated to the worship of the goddess Earth. As time passed, other deities were included in the cult: Poseidon, Themis. Guardian of Earth's oracle was her son, the dragon Python.

As an infant, only a few days old, Apollo started from Delos, the place of his birth, in search of a suitable place for the erection of his temple. He crossed Pieria, Euboea, Boeotia, and stopped at the Telfoussa spring in Aliartos; deceived by the nymph Telfoussa who was mistress of the region, however, he left the place and climbed the hill-sides of Mt. Parnassus eventually reaching Delphi. According to the Homeric Hymn to Apollo – an important literary document – the site pleased the god, and he decided to have his temple there. But taking possession of the place was no easy matter. Using his arrows and a lighted torch, Apollo killed Python, the guardian of Earth's oracle.

First priests at the temple – again according to the Hymn – became some Cretan merchants who happened to be sailing from Cnossos to Pylos. By a miracle, Apollo made their ship deviate from its route and come to Cirrha, the port of Krissa. From there, the god led the sailors to *Pytho* – the ancient name of Delphi by which it is referred to in the Hymn.

The cult of the goddess Earth was not entirely driven out of Delphi. A small, unadorned place was left to her at the site where her oracle had stood, and there the original mistress of the area continued to be worshipped.

The new master of the Delphic oracle brought a new spirit with him – the spirit, in fact, that was to dominate the social and political life of the Greeks for centuries to come. In Delphi more than anywhere else was the cult of Apollo permeated by the peaceable and spiritual nature of the god who always tried to reconcile conflicting interests and bring humaneness to prevailing customs. The god himself set the example. Having killed Python, he self-exiled himself from Olympus and went to the Tempe Valley; in order to cleanse himself from the murder, he entered the service of king Admetus of Ferai as a slave and worked as a shepherd for the royal flocks. Purified, Apollo returned to Delphi crowned with laurels from Tempe.

Little by little, Apollo became to all men, individuals as well as cities, the god of purification, the god who provided right answers to problems through the oracular responses given by his sanctuary. The oracle did much towards softening the mores and eliminating cruel practices, such as revenge requiring a life for a life. It also encouraged colonialism as a means of attenuating the causes of strife between the small city-states of ancient Greece. It was no accidental fact that the temple bore inscriptions of the dicta of the Seven Sages advising moderation in all aspects of human life.

Apollo was also closely connected with the arts. He was the god of music and poetry and the Muses were his constant companions. The guitar, given to him at his birth together with the bow, had the power to appease superhuman influences. It is significant that the Pythian Games owed their glory and prestige mainly to musical and poetic contests, unlike the Olympic Games where athletic competition predominated.

For all these qualities that the god personified, the Greeks were grateful to him. After every victory, every great achievement, or deliverance from calamity or disease, they would come to Apollo with their gifts – an entire building, a treasury, statues made of precious metals and many other offerings.

The Pythia: The will of Apollo was expressed at Delphi by the Pythia, a venerated woman of Delphi. In the early years, the Pythia was young and a virgin. Later it was ruled that she had to be more than 50 years old. She lived in the sanctuary of Apollo and her life had to be irreproachable in every respect. In the oracle's heyday, there were three Pythias, in its decline, when hardly anyone consulted it any more, this number was reduced to one.

For Pythia to give an answer, both she and the applicants (*theopropoi*, as they were called) had to follow a strictly regulated procedure: first the theopropoi cleansed themselves with the water of the Castalia spring, paid a fee *(pelanos)* which differed from case to case, and sacrificed an animal, usually a kid, on the altar of Apollo. The animal had to be perfect, i.e. free from any defect. Before the sacrifice, cold water was poured over the animal. As a sign that the god was at home and the day was convenient, the animal had to start trembling all over. That was an unmistakable indication that the day was propitious and an answer could be obtained.

In the early period of the oracle, oracular responses were given once a year, on the 7th day of the month of Vyssios (February–March), which was Apollo's birthday. As the oracle's popularity increased, this rule was changed, and answers were given on the 7th day of each month except the three winter months when Apollo, according to tradition, left Delphi and went to the Hyperboraeans (the Nordic peoples). During these months, Delphi was given over to the worship of Dionysus, celebrated by feasting in the sanctuary and on Mt. Parnassus.

Had the sacrifice proved propitious, the Pythia entered the temple, after she and the priests (or prophets) who were to attend the giving of the answer had also cleansed themselves with the water of the Castalia; then she proceeded to burn laurel and barley flour on the hearth where the immortal fire was kept. Following this she descended to the underground adyton *(antron)* beneath the nave of the temple, while the priests and the applicants waited in another small enclosure, the *oikos* (house). From this *oikos* the applicant asked his question in a clear and loud voice.

The Pythia drank water from the Cassotis spring which flowed through the underground shrine (see p. 19), chewed laurel leaves and mounted on the sacred tripod which stood by the «umbilicus» (*omphalos* = navel), or just touched it while inhaling the *spirit* emanating from the gap (probably some fissure in the earth), and fell into a trance. Then she began to speak, while the priests wrote down and interpreted her words. The answers were given either in verse or in prose.

The Oracles: The oracles written down by the priests from the meaningless (for laymen) utterances of Pythia, constituted the real power of the sanctuary. From the 6th century on, «the oracle was acknowledged throughout the Greek world as the arbitrator and safeguarder of right faith and right thinking: In every crisis, it was the oracle that decreed which god or which hero would avert a calamity or ensure a success; without its consent, no cult was instituted in any city no existing institution was changed, no new institution was introduced».*

Pythia's answers are known from literary sources, mainly Herodotus in the earlier period, and from inscriptions. The earlier answers, delivered in Homeric hexameters, have become famous for their cryptic or ambiguous meaning often leading to doubt or misunderstanding. One typical example is the answer given to Croesus during his war against Cyrus:

> If Croesus crosses the river Aly, he will destroy a great kingdom.

And so he did, only the kingdom he destroyed was not Cyrus's as he had thought, but his own kingdom of Lydia. Apollo did not lie to him, but he simply gave an ambiguous answer, well in keeping with the god's typical indirectness, so well known to the Greeks, that it was used as one of his attributes (*Loxias*). In one of his preserved passages, the philosopher Heracleitus explains and justifies this quality of the god: *The master to whom the oracle at Delphi belongs neither reveals the truth nor conceals it, he only gives signs* (i.e. for the party concerned to interpret).

The impact and power of the oracle was at its highest during the 7th and 6th c. B.C. It was the period in which the Greeks began to feel restricted by the narrow confines of their homeland and to look around for new places where they could be free from political pressures. So before starting on their journey to the unknown far-off points around the Mediterranean basin where they intended to found a new colony, the chiefs of the colonizing missions (the *oikistai*) came to consult Apollo about the prospects of success of their enterprise, and about the place that was to be their new home. It has been said and is probably true that the oracle had precise information concerning areas which lent themselves to colonization around the Mediterranean; the Etruscans who often visited Delphi were probably the main source of such information. So when Vattos from Thera was advised by Pythia to colonize Libya but he, not daring to land on the African mainland, had colonized an island – Plataea – off the African coast instead, and then came back to ask why his colony did not seem to thrive, he received this answer from Pythia:

> If thou, not having been there, knowest sheep-rearing Libya better than I, who have been there do, then I must admire thy wisdom.

The colonies established by advice from the Delphic oracle recognized Apollo as their patron (*archegetes*) and many were named Apollonia after the god.

The oracular responses of Delphi were a means of appeasing the blazing passions of the growing-up period of ancient Greece. Apollo indicated how far man could go without crossing over the limits set by deity. «The Delphic oracle did not deny its consent to the aristocratic government of Lycurgus, which meant abolition of the autocratic rule of the kings, nor to the republic of Cleisthenes, which meant abolition of aristocratic clans. But in every case, directly or indirectly, it recommended moderation and humility»**.

It should not be thought, however, that the oracle adopted invariably a correct or impartial attitude. Through the Pythia's answers, it often undisguisedly sided with one party or threw its moral weight with a cause that might benefit some to the detriment of others. During the Persian Wars, it wavered at first under the shock of the Persian invasion, and

---

* P. DE LA COSTE - MESSELIÈRE
** CHR. KAROUSOS

adopted a policy that might well have shaken the confidence of the Greeks who were defending their fatherland. But after the Persians had been driven back, it was to Delphi again that the Greeks came to fetch the sacred flame wherewith to light again their altar fires extinguished by the barbarians. During the Peloponnesian War, the oracle openly espoused the cause of the Lacedemonians by the answer it gave when asked by the latter whether they would win.

Oracular responses were given to applicants in a certain predetermined order. First came the citizens of Delphi and then those who had been honoured by the town of Delphi with the right of precedence *(promanteia)* (see p. 18, inscription on the altar of the Chians). If there were several applicants holding right of precedence, the order in which they received their answers was drawn by lot. Last came those not belonging to one of the above groups, in an order also drawn by lot.

The Treasuries: As the visitor will see at the sanctuary of Apollo, the small buildings known as treasuries were numerous. Of most of these, only the foundations or insignificant remnants can be seen at present. But there are some from which something more has been preserved – either parts of their architecture or fragments of their sculptural decoration. The restored treasury of the Athenians is a fine example of this type of buildings. Their form was typical, not only at Delphi but in sanctuaries all over Greece, e.g. Olympia and Delos: they were small in size (the treasury of the Athenians measures 8.61 m. in length, 6.52 m. in width and 7.59 m. in height) and most had two columns between two door-posts in their façade. The treasury of Siphnos had two female statues – Caryatids – instead of columns, parts of which can be seen in the museum.

The main purpose of these treasuries was safe keeping of the ex-votoes offered the sanctuary by the city concerned, and their protection against the weather. But they were often indirectly used as a means of extolling some important feat, usually a war victory. So the treasury of the Athenians was erected from the spoils of the Battle of Marathon and its sculptural decoration symbolised the victory of the Athenians over the Persians; the treasury of Syracuse, on the other hand, standing right across the way from that of Athens, perpetuated the memory of the Syracusans' victory when they defeated the Athenians at Sicily in 413 B.C. Unlike these two examples, the treasury of Siphnos was a display of wealth and luxury, intended to impress visitors to Delphi. The position of the various treasuries within the precinct depended on the wealth and power commanded by the offering city and was an indication of the amount of influence the city concerned could wield at the oracle.

The Excavations of Delphi: The ruins of Delphi were brought to light by the excavations carried out first by the French School of Archaeology from 1892 onwards, under Théophile Homolle in the early years. Over the ruins of the sanctuary of Apollo stood then the village of Delphi – known by the local name «Kastri». The village was expropriated and rebuilt at its present site.

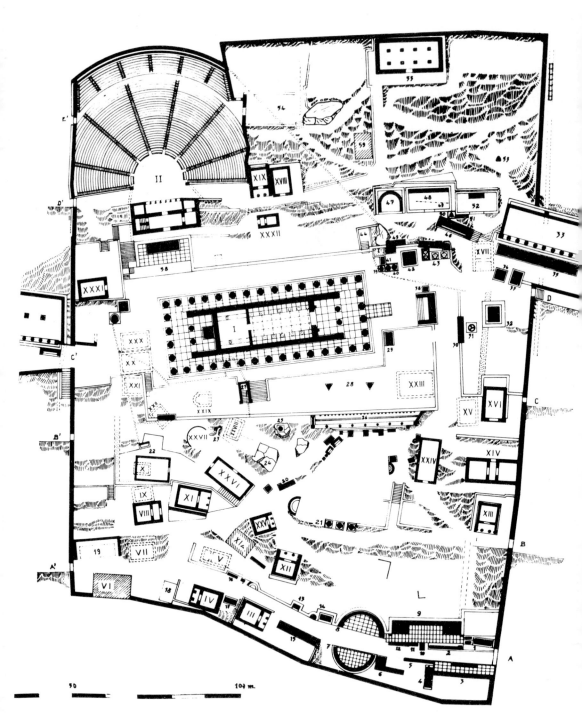

Topographical plan of the sanctuary of Apollo (J. Pouilloux - G. Roux).

General view of the sanctuary of Apollo.

THE RUINS OF DELPHI

The Sanctuary of the Pythian Apollo: The sanctuary of Apollo is situated at the foot of Rho‗ dhini – one of the two Phedriads – and it was surrounded in antiquity by an enclosure, a wall, which precluded entrance on all sides. There were several major and minor gates in this wall, which are marked on the drawing of the sanctuary, but the main entrance was the one now situated a little above the public thoroughfare between the museum and the Castalia spring. This entrance marks the starting point of the *Sacred Way* and still gives access to the shrine.

In front of the main entrance to the sanctuary, there is a large rectangular paved square, which in ancient times was flanked by Ionic order porticoes with shops at the far end. Some remnants of these porticoes are visible on the northern side of the square. This aggregate of structures represents an *agora* (marketplace) built in Roman times for the purpose of supplying pilgrims visiting the sanctuary with offerings for the god (statuettes, small tripods), and other religious objects.

The square also served, at least in later years, as a place of assembly for the magnificent processions organised on the occasion of the sanctuary's festivals. Scattered over the square are still some pedestals on which stood statues of Roman emperors or other persons of note (Pl. 49).

The Sacred Way starts from Gate A of the shrine and follows a crooked course to the temple. It lies today at a lower level than in antiquity; the pavement dates from a later period, when the sanctuary of Apollo had become an insignificant village of the Byzantine era. Lining the Sacred Way on either side were various offerings to Apollo and the treasuries whose splendour aroused the admiration of ascending visitors.

The first monument, on the right of the Sacred Way, is part of the large base of a bronze bull (**1**), the work of the sculptor Theopropos of Aegina, dedicated by the inhabitants of Corfu around the year 480 B.C. and representing one-tenth of their proceeds from a miraculous catch of tuna fish for which a bull was responsible. The story is told by Pausanias, and an identical offering existed at Olympia.

The Bull of Corfu (Reconstruction by H. Pomtow).

At a small distance from the base of the bull, there is another base (**2**) which supported nine bronze statues dedicated by the Arcadians from the spoils of their victorious campaign under Epameinondas against the Spartans in Laconia in 370-369 B.C. The statues represented gods, heroes and heroines of Arcadia: Apollo, Nike (Victory), Kallisto, Arcas, Apheidas, Elatos, Azanus, Triphylos and Erassos.

Across from this offering of the Arcadians (**3**), according to Pausanias, i.e. on the left side of the Sacred Way, the Spartans had erected 37 bronze statues after their glorious victory against the Athenians at Aegos Potamoi in 404 B.C. Some of these statues represented the victor Lysander being crowned by Poseidon, the Dioscuri, Zeus, Apollo, Artemis, and the generals and admirals of the Spartans at that great sea-battle. The arrogance and impertinence of this offering contrasted sharply with the dignity of the monument commemorating the Athenian victory at Marathon, which stood on its right.

Beside the statues of the «admirals», as the monumental offering of the Lacedemonians is known, stood a bronze Trojan Horse (**4**), the work of the Argive sculptor Antiphanes, offered by the Argives to Apollo from the spoils taken from the Spartans at the battle at Thyreatis in 414 B.C.

In the space in front of the Trojan Horse, always according to Pausanias's description, the Athenians had erected 16 statues (**5**) representing Athene, Apollo, the victor of the Battle of Marathon Miltiades, and 7 heads of Athenian tribes. These statues, the work of Phidias, represented one-tenth of the spoils of the Battle of Marathon and were offered at a much later date, perhaps under Cimon, when Miltiades's honour had been restored. Many years later, likenesses of the kings Antigonus, Demetrius and Ptolemy of Egypt, patrons of new Attic tribes, were added to the monument.

By the side of the Trojan Horse to the west, there stood another offering by the Argives, consisting of a group of statues (**6**) representing the seven mythical chiefs who had marched against Thebes in order to depose Eteocles. The groups included the chariot of Amphiaraos with the hero and his charioteer Vato on it. The group was the work of the sculptors Hypatodorus and Aristogeiton and represented one-tenth of the booty from the battle fought between the Argives and the Lacedemonians at Oenoe of Argolis in 456 B.C.

In the semicircular (**7**) space flanking the above group, the Argives again had erected the statues of the Seven Epigoni, i.e. the sons of the *Seven against Thebes,* who had launched a new attack on the same city and had captured and destroyed it. According to the form of the letters of the inscription *(the Argives offered to Apollo),* this offering dates from the second quarter of the 5th century B.C. and according to Pausanias, the funds used for its making also came from the spoils of the battle of Oenoe (456 B.C.).

Exactly opposite the Epigoni, another semicircular recess has been preserved (**8**) where the Argives, after the foundation of Messene in 369 B.C. in cooperation with the Thebans and Epameinondas, had erected 10 bronze statues of heroes and kings; the first represented Danaus, the most powerful king of Argos, followed by the statue of Hypermnestra and others, who together made up the Argive family from which Hercules was descended. The last two statues in the series were those of Alcmene and Hercules. In dedicating this offering which was the work of the Argive sculptor Antiphanes, the Argives had intended to underline the ties existing between Argos and its then powerful ally Thebes. Hercules, who was of Argive parentage but Theban by birth, symbolised the friendship which had developed between the two cities after 370 B.C.

East of the semicircle of the Argive kings and heroes, there is a large rectangular recess (**9**). Some archaeologists believe that its purpose was to accommodate the large offering of the Spartans (**3**), but this is in contradiction both with Pausanias and with the findings of recent archaeological research.

The Tholos of Sicyon (Reconstruction by H. Pomtow).

In front of the latter recess, there are the remnants of a pedestal (**10**) which supported a bronze statue of the general of the Achaean League Philopoemen. High in the front of this pedestal is the votive inscription : *The Achaean League* (dedicated this statue of) *Philopoemen son of Kraugius of Megalopoli in recognition of his valour and of his services to them.* Plutarch relates that Philopoemen was pictured in the posture in which he had killed the tyrant of Sparta Machanidas in battle in 207 B.C.

Returning again to the opposite side of the Sacred Way, we can see to the west of the semicircle of the Epigoni, the vestiges of a large base (**15**) which, according to Pausanias, supported an offering by the city of Taras: bronze statues of horses and captive women, made from the loot of a victorious battle fought by the Tarantines against their barbarian neighbours, the Messapians. The statues were the work of the great sculptor Ageladas (first quarter of the 5th c. B.C.).

The building of porous stone (**III**), remnants of which can be seen to the west of the offering of Taras is the treasury of Sicyon (Pl. 49). In the introduction, we have briefly discussed the purpose and the general form of the treasuries. This particular treasury, of Doric order with two columns between two door posts *(antae)* on its façade, was erected around 500 B.C. by the oligarchic party who had deposed the tyrants of Sicyon, the Orthagoridae. What is of particular importance in connection with this treasury is the fact that at its foundation, used as building materials, were found remnants of two older porous stone buildings erected by the Sicyonians at Delphi: One was a round peripteral structure with 13 Doric columns, 6.32 m. in diameter, resembling in form the tholos of the sanctuary of Athene Pronaia and built around 580 B.C. at the site of the ancient shrine of goddess Earth; much later, Herodes Atticus erected his *exedra* on the same spot. The second building, of which some structural parts and metope reliefs were found, was small and rectangular (4.182 m. × 5.475 m.) built in the style called *monopteron* by the ancients, i.e. consisting only of a colonnade (14 small Doric columns) with a roof *(pteron)* without inner walls. This building dates from approx. 560 B.C. and the purpose it served is unknown. According to one hypothesis, it housed the chariot of Cleisthenes, tyrant of Sicyon, who won at the chariot races of the first Pythian Games held in 582 B.C. The metopes, which are of great interest for the history of archaic plastic art, will be discussed in the part dealing with the museum.

Next to the treasury of Sicyon stood the treasury of Siphnos (**IV**), the most beautiful and sumptuous building in the sanctuary of Apollo. Built around 525 B.C. from marble of Paros, of the Ionic order, it had two female statues – Caryatids – instead of columns in front, was richly decorated with sculptures, pediments with sculptured scenes and a continuous frieze, the remnants of which will be seen at the museum. This treasury did not commemorate any victory or other important event in the history of Siphnos. According to Herodotus and Pausanias, it was built from one-tenth of the proceeds of the gold mines of the island and its purpose was to impress the other Greeks with its splendour; and this purpose it seems to have been achieved, since even Herodotus described it as extremely rich.

The treasury of Siphnos
(Reconstruction by W. B. Dinsmoor).

The treasury of Siphnos brings the visitor to the «crossroads of the treasuries». A little to the west, there are the remains of the lovely treasury of Thebes (**VI**), built after the battle of Leuctra (371 B.C.) with local stone, the treasury of Boeotia (**VII**) made of porous stone, and another treasury which is believed to have been erected by the city of Potidaea (**VIII**). The corner opposite the treasury of Siphnos is supported by a retaining wall inscribed with various decrees concerning inhabitants of Megara. On the strength of this evidence it is believed that the treasury of Megara (**V**) stood on the terrace formed by this wall.

The treasury of the Athenians (**XI**), made of Paros marble (restored in 1903–1906 with funds allocated by the City of Athens), is a sample of the beauty of these buildings. As it rises, in its actual dimensions, from the Delphic scenery, this restored treasury must convey to the modern onlooker the same impression as its original did in ancient times (Pl. 50).

The treasury was erected in 490–489 B.C. from one-tenth of the proceeds of the spoils of the Battle of Marathon and, besides being an offering in itself, it was intended to house other offerings of the Athenians to the god. In terms of architecture and sculpture, it represents the transition from archaic style to the severe style of Attic art.

The building is of the Doric order with two columns between two door-posts on the eastern side; it was ornamented with sculptured pediments (representing, perhaps, Theseus meeting Peirithous on the front side, and a battle scene on the western side), and sculptured metopes. In the front, i.e. the eastern side of the treasury, six metopes represented a battle of the Ama-

TRESOR
DES ATHENIENS

FACADE PRINCIPALE

TRESOR
DES ATHENIENS

The treasury of the Athenians (Reconstruction by A. Tournaire).

zons, the whole symbolising (after the recent triumph at Marathon) the successful struggle against the barbarian invader, the common enemy of all the Greeks. On the southern side, 9 metopes depicted various feats of Theseus, the national hero of Athens. Another 9 metopes along the northern side of the building told of Hercules's labours, while on the rear, i.e. the western side, 6 further metopes depicted still another labour of Hercules, the steeling of the oxen of Geryon. The 24 best preserved metopes are kept in the museum. The ones on the present building are plaster reproductions of the originals.

From the 3rd century B.C. onwards, the walls of the treasury were inscribed upon with various texts, such as decrees honouring Athenians. On the southern wall, two hymns to Apollo were inscribed and will be seen in the museum. Inscriptions can also be seen on the wall fencing off to the north the small square in front of the treasury.

The treasury of the Athenians remained intact almost until modern times. At the last it had become a house of pawnbrokers as can be seen from the names scratched on the wall to mark each pawnbroker's place.

On the left of the treasury there is a triangular space where the Athenians had placed actual spoils from the Battle of Marathon, as announced by the large sign at its front: *The Athenians to Apollo from the spoils of the Persians at the Battle of Marathon.*

A lengthy, archaic, porous stone building next to the treasury of Athens (**XXVI**), was the Parliament (Bouleuterion), where the 15 representatives and the 8 aldermen (*prytaneis*) of Delphi held their meetings. Across from this was the treasury of Syracuse (**XIA**) erected after the great victory of the Syracusans against the Athenians in 413 B.C. The position of this building is significant: to better set off the magnitude of their triumph, the Syracusans erected their treasury opposite that of Athens.The Arcadians did the same later, when they set their offering (**2**) opposite the monument commemorating the sea-battle at Aigos Potamoi (**3**). The treasury of Syracuse was Doric and only its façade had triglyphs and metopes. Some fine members of this building – a corner triglyph of black stone and a white marble cornice – will be seen in the roofed space outside the museum.

Next to the treasury of Syracuse, there was the treasury of Cnidos (**XXV**), of the Ionic order, with fine architectural sculptural ornamentation, built after the middle of the 6th century B.C. To the north of it, there was a semicircular platform with statues.

The large rock to the right of the Parliament had at some very early time fallen from the Phedriads and was known – according to Plutarch and Pausanias – as the Stone of Sibyl, because according to tradition, the first Sibyl, Herophile, had stood on it to deliver her oracles and stood there whenever she came to Delphi; for this first Sibyl, the Delphic Sibyl as she came to be known, was not a native of Delphi like the other Pythias. Tradition has it that Herophile had predicted the Trojan War.

The narrow pass between the Parliament and the Stone of Sibyl leads to a now dry fountain (**23**). That was the spring guarded by the great dragon Python, Earth's son, whom Apollo had to kill before he could take possession of the sanctuary. This part, then, of the sanctuary of Apollo, i.e. the part beyond the Stone of Sibyl, is the site where in times immemorial Earth and the deities of subterranean waters, the Muses, were worshipped. Later, Themis the goddess of divine justice, and Poseidon were worshipped at the same place. This very ancient sanctuary was almost entirely destroyed after 548 B.C., when extensive construction work and especially the building of the polygonal wall were undertaken.

The arch beside the spring (**XXVII**) is what remains of an exedra built by the rich Athenian sophist Herodes Atticus at the site of the former porous stone tholos of Sicyon, while the fountain further west (**22**) belonged to a small shrine of Aesculapius the corresponding temple being perhaps the structure which had been erected to the south of the fountain upon the ruins of an archaic treasury (**X**).

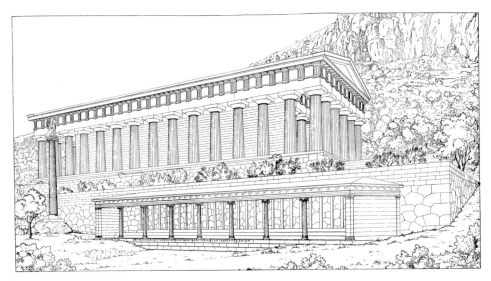

The Stoa of the Athenians and the temple of the «Alcmeonidae» (Reconstruction by P. Amandry).

To the right of the Stone of Sibyl, there is another, smaller, rock. On this, according to tradition, Leto stood holding the infant Apollo in her arms, while he trained his arrow on Python. On the rock beyond, stood the Sphinx of Naxos, which can be seen in the museum. The marble drums lying around are from the tall column of the sphinx.

To the right of the rocks, a circular space is formed which the ancients called *Halos* (a threshing floor). There, every 8 years, a religious drama, the *Septerion*, was acted out reproducing the killing of Python by Apollo. A child whose parents must both be alive acted the part of Apollo. The priests led the child up a staircase called *Doloneia* to a hut in the Halos to shoot the dragon who was hiding there. Then the child madebelieve he was going to Tempe to atone for the murder as the god had done.

The large wall fencing off the area of the Halos to the north-west is the famous polygonal wall, built after the destruction of the temple in 548 B.C. as a reinforcement of the ground where the new temple (that of the Alcmeonidae) was to be erected. It is of interest to note that the joints between the perfectly fitted stones are curved. The mode of construction is an elaborate form of the so-called *Lesbian* form of building (Pl. 51). The whole surface of the wall is covered with various inscriptions, mainly deeds of liberation of slaves, some 800 in number.

In front of the eastern half of the wall, there was an Ionic order portico (**26**) with seven monolithic columns of Pentelic marble (except the capitals and the bases which were of Paros marble), supporting a wooden entablature and roof. This was built by the Athenians after 478 B.C. to house naval trophies from Athenian victories (Pl. 51). On the face of the *stylobate*, there is a large votive inscription: *The Athenians offered the portico and the arms and the acroteria captured from the enemy*. According to the findings of modern archaeological research, the *arms* referred to in the inscription were the ropes used to fasten the bridges over the Hellespont which had enabled Xerxes and his army to cross the water and invade Greece, while the *acroteria* were figure-heads of Persian ships. These and other trophies from subsequent Athenian victories were kept in the portico.

Surrounding the Halos were other important buildings as well; there was an Aeolic order treasury (**XII**), perhaps of Klazomenai, the treasury of Cyrene (**XIII**), the building supposed to have been the Prytanaeum (**XIV**), and the treasury of Corinth (**XXIV**) which was built by the tyrant of Corinth Kypselos (657–628 B.C.), father of Periandros, and which was the oldest treasury in Delphi. After the destruction of the temple of Apollo in 548 B.C., all valuable offerings rescued from the destruction were moved into the treasury of Corinth. Some of them were of legendary value: the throne of Midas, king of Phrygia, the six gold kraters (mixing bowls) of Gyges, the gold lion of Croesus resting on a base consisting of 117 gold plinths, precious statues, invaluable vases. Herodotus, the historian, saw many of these offerings in the treasury, which still existed at the time of Plutarch and Pausanias, though by then it was of course empty.

Continuing along the Sacred Way after the bend it forms at the treasury of Corinth, we meet, on the left, the large altar constructed by the Chians at their own expense in the 5th century B.C., as attested by the inscription shown high up on the cornice of the altar: *The Chians to Apollo, this altar* (Pl. 53). Another inscription at the base of the altar says: *Delphi granted the right of promanteia to the Chians*, meaning the exceptional privilege of receiving oracles from Pythia immediately after the citizens of Delphi. The altar, made of white marble in its upper and lower parts while the rest is made of dark marble, presents a pleasing bichromatic contrast in addition to its harmonious proportions. Next to the altar on the northern side, there stood a tall column (**38**) bearing a statue of Eumenes II king of Pergamon, an offering of the Aetolians, with an artfully engraved inscription, which will be seen in the roofed space outside the museum. Another high column (**29**) in front of the southeastern corner

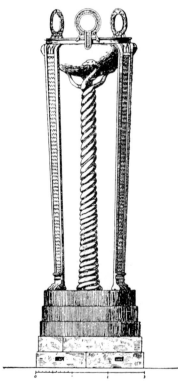

The Tripod of Plataea. Reconstruction
(Furtwängler - Bulle)

of the temple had been erected to receive the statue of king Perseus of Macedonia, but as fate would have it, it was eventually used to support the statue of the Roman general Aemilius Paulus who defeated Perseus at Pydna in 168 B.C. The reliefs of this column, showing scenes from the Battle of Pydna, can be seen outside the museum.

Opposite the altar, at a somewhat lower level, are the remnants of one of the most highly respected monuments in the history of Greece: the Tripod of Plataea. What remains of it now is only the base (Pl. 51) on which stood the gold cauldron and the three coiled up bronze snakes among the legs of the tripod (**31**). This offering was made from one-tenth of the spoils of the Battle of Plataea (479 B.C.) and on the three reptiles were engraved the names of the cities that had fought together against the Persians at that battle. The three snakes were taken to Constantinople by Constantine the Great and are now displayed there in the Hippodrome Square.

In front of the base of the Tripod of Plataea can be seen parts of another pedestal which supported an offering of Taras, and behind it there stood a gold chariot of the Sun, dedicated by Rhodes (**32**). Further north and preserved to a considerable height, there is a portico (**33**) built by Attalus I the Saviour, king of Pergamon (241–197 B.C.); it is of the Doric order and has 11 columns on the front side. Standing in parallel to the façade of the portico, there was a large base presumably supporting some important offering by Attalus. In Roman times, the portico was closed by a wall joining the columns and used as a water reservoir serving the thermae (baths) situated outside the precinct, to the southeast of the portico.

In front of the portico, there were two tall pillars (**36-37**) supporting statues of Attalus I and Eumenes II (197–160 B.C.).

An important region is the area west of the portico (Stoa) of Attalus, which, in antiquity, was filled with precious offerings. The large base (**46**) probably bore an offering by the citizens of Corfu, and the rectangular space behind it (**52**) is the shrine of Neoptolemus, son of Achilles. According to the legend, Neoptolemus was killed at Delphi by the priest of Apollo and this shrine was believed to include his grave.

On the porous stone base (**50**), one side of which is engraved with the letters PAN (short form of *Pancrates*, a well-known contractor at Delphi) probably stood the high floral column with the three graceful dancers – an offering of the Athenians, now kept in the museum. Inside the precinct, on the left side, there was an offering by Daochus II, a tetrarch of Thessaly and hieromnemon at Delphi from 336 to 332 B.C. One can still see the long base with the nine cavities into which the nine statues of Daochus's offering to Apollo were fitted. These statues represented members of Daochus's family and on the front side of the base, the inscriptions (mostly in verse) which accompanied each statue are easily legible. The 6 best preserved of the nine statues can be seen in the museum.

The nearby horseshoe-shaped base (**47**) supported a similar offering consisting of at least 17 statues of the early Hellenistic period.

Coming back to the Sacred Way after this brief digression, we find two bell-shaped pedestals (**43**). According to literary evidence as well as to the inscriptions engraved on them, they bore gold tripods and «Victories», offerings of Gelon tyrant of Syracuse, and Hieron his brother, sons of Deinomenes, in commemoration of their victory against the Carthaginians at Himera in 479 B.C. It has been said that «both the type of offering (tripods) and its location indicated that the ancients themselves saw a parallelism between Himera, Salamis and Plataea»*. Next to the base of Gelon, there is another, smaller pedestal; a fourth pedestal is between the polygonal wall and the temple. It is postulated that the third and fourth pedestal bore tripods of gold dedicated by Gelon's two other brothers, Thrasybule and Polyzalus; this theory gains additional credibility from an ode by the great poet Bacchylides.

To the left of the bases of the Deinomenidae, there were other important offerings, such as the statue of Apollo Sitalcas (**42**) which was 15.50 m. high; the offering of Aristaeneta (**40**) resting on two Ionic columns and the tall pillar of Prussias II, king of Bithynia (182–149 B.C.) with his statue on top, dedicated by the Aetolian League as indicated by the inscription engraved on the upper part of the pedestal (pl. 52). In front of Prussias's pillar there is a foundation on which stood the bronze palm-tree with the gold Athene offered by the Athenians for their victory against the Persians at the River Eurymedon in the 5th century B.C. – an offering comparable to the bronze sail with three gold stars dedicated in pursuance of an oracle by the citizens of Aegina for their outstanding contribution to victory at the sea-battle of Salamis.

The water of the Cassotis spring played an important role in the soothsaying function. Recent research has shown that the spring was situated almost immediately behind Prussias's pillar. A narrow staircase between the wall which is a continuation of the *Ischegaon* and a water reservoir, led to a second reservoir, and that is where the Cassotis is now known to have been (**44**).

---

* CHR. KAROUSOS

The 4th-century-B.C. temple of Apollo (Reconstruction by H. Schleif).

We are now facing the ruins of the most important building in the sanctuary of Apollo: the ruins of the temple (I). Everything that can be seen at present belonged to the last (known from archaeological research) temple of the god, which dates from the 4th century B.C. (Pl. 53). Other temples had preceded this last one on the same spot. The ancients believed that the first temple was made of laurel; it was probably a simple fence or a roof made from intertwined laurel branches. The second temple was made of bee-wax and wings, the third was of bronze, the fourth was the one built, according to ancient tradition, by the legendary architects Trophonius and Agamedes and known from the Homeric Hymn to Apollo. It was a porous stone structure, of the Doric order and some of its remnants have been excavated and dated to approx. 650 B.C. The fourth temple was destroyed by fire in 548 B.C. Money for the construction of the new temple came from all over Greece as well as from foreign princes, and by 510 B.C. the temple was complete. It became known as the temple of the Alcmeonidae, because the Alcmeonidae, noble Athenians exiled by the tyrant Peisistratus, had acted as contractors for its construction (see p. 39). There were 6 columns at the front and 15 along the lateral sides. Instead of the porous stone stipulated by their contract, the Alcmeonidae – hoping to win the favour of the sanctuary in their effort to overthrow Peisistratus – used Paros marble on the eastern façade and in the sculptures of the eastern pediment. An earthquake in 373 B.C. reduced the temple to ruins. The sanctuary launched a second appeal for a panhellenic collection for its rebuilding but the Second Sacred War delayed the construction work so that the temple was not fully operative until 330 B.C. It had

The façade of the temple of the «Alcmeonidae» (Reconstruction by F. Courby).

the same design and nearly the same dimension as the temple of the Alcmeonidae; porous stone was used for the columns and the entablature, while the rest of the temple was made from the lovely dark stone of Mt. Parnassus. The architects were first Spintharus of Corinth and, after his death, Xenodorus and Agathon. The pediments were made by the Athenian sculptors Praxias and Androsthenes. According to Pausanias, the eastern pediment represented the god's *epiphany* i.e. arrival at Delphi (like the eastern pediment of the temple of the Alcmeonidae which will be seen in the museum together with the western pediment made of porous stone); the western pediment of the new temple represented Dionysus between the Maenads (Thyiads) and the setting sun. The metopes of the temple bore no representations but Persian shields from the Battle of Marathon and Gallic shields from the Gaul invasion of Delphi (279 B.C.) were attached to them.

From descriptions of ancient writers, a few things are known about the internal arrangement of the temple. The walls of the pronaos (vestibule) were engraved with precepts of the Seven Sages, such as *Know Thyself* and *Nothing to Excess* and with the letter *E*, the significance of which is still unknown. Plutarch wrote a whole treatise in an – unsuccessful – effort to interpret this *E*. Also in the pronaos there was a bronze representation of Homer and inscribed on its base was an oracle that had been given to the poet.

The nave seems to have been divided into two parts. In the front part there was an altar of Poseidon, the predecessor of Apollo in the sanctuary, statues of the two Fates (Moirae), of Zeus Moiragetas and Apollo Moiragetas, the iron throne on which Pindar sat when he came to Delphi and sang hymns to Apollo, and the hearth upon which Neoptolemus, the son of Achilles, was killed by the priest of Apollo. Pausanias wrote that few people were entitled to enter the second part of the nave, and that it contained a gold statue of Apollo.

The large retaining wall to the north of the temple is the so-called *Ischegaon* (*ischo* = to retain + *gan* = earth) known from the accounts concerning the construction of the 4th-c.-temple (from 356 B.C. on). The half-destroyed recess still visible in this wall was intended to accomodate the statue of some important person.

Continuing on our way parallel to the Ischegaon, we come to a large rectangular recess (**58**). Here Crateros, son of that other Crateros who was a general of Alexander the Great, had placed after 320 B.C. a group of bronze statues – works of the great sculptors Lysippus and Leochares – representing, according to Plutarch's description, hunting hounds, Alexander at grips with a lion, and general Crateros running to his rescue. High up on the wall at the far end of the recess, an epigram is inscribed mentioning the dedicator and the incident represented by the group of statues.

Before proceeding to the theatre, we may for a moment deviate from our course and leave the sanctuary through Gate C'in order to look at another large portico. Like the S t o a of Attalos, it was intended to offer visitors to the sanctuary an opportunity to walk or rest while being sheltered from the weather. Owing to its size, this portico had two colonnades, an inner one along the longitudinal axis of the building, and an outer one along the façade.

To the left of the recess of Crateros's offering, a steep flight of stairs leads to the theatre (II) of the sanctuary, one of the best preserved ancient theatres in Greece (Pl. 54). Built of white Parnassus stone in the 4th century B.C., it is divided into two parts: the *koilon* (hollow) with 35 rows of semicircular seats for the spectators, and the stage. The lower part of the koilon is divided by flights of stairs into seven tiers, while the upper part is divided into six tiers. Between the upper and lower part there is a gangway called *diazoma*.

The recess with the offering of Crateros (Reconstruction by F. Courby).

The Theatre of Delphi (Reconstruction by H. Schleif).

The theatre was repaired in the 2nd century B.C.· there is in fact an inscription in the sanctuary mentioning that the king of Pergamon Eumenes II sent money and slaves to Delphi for the repair of the theatre. In the 1st century A.D., a frieze was placed in front of the stage representing in relief various scenes from the labours of Hercules; the frieze is now kept in the museum.

The orchestra is paved and there is an open ditch for rainwater running around it. The stage is divided into two sections: there is the proscenium in front consisting of three divisions, and the stage proper at the rear also consisting of three divisions. The stage was rather low so as not to obstruct the exquisite view of the Delphic landscape with the two Phedriads, the valley of the Pleistos and Mt. Kirphys on the opposite side.

The theatre has an estimated capacity of approximately 5,000 persons. It was regularly used during the great festivals of the sanctuary but was not continuously in operation. From various inscriptions it is known that lectures and recitals of poetry were presented at the gymnasium, while musical performances were given in the stadium. The ancients used the theatre mainly for dramatic and lyrical contests.

Being a place where large crowds gathered, the theatre naturally served for purposes of publicity: official deeds concerning almost exclusively liberation of slaves were inscribed in abundance on the pilasters of the orchestra and on the walls of side entrances (parodoi).

The last monument to be seen inside the sanctuary is what remains of the renowned Lesche of Cnidos (55). There is no certainty as to its exact form but in a general way it was a hypostyle hall with a roof supported by two rows of 4 wooden posts. The entrance was on the southern side. Inside, there was a continuous bench along the walls for habitués to sit on. The Lesche was a meeting place and discussion forum.

What makes the Lesche of Cnidos important is that its four walls were decorated on the inside with paintings by the great ancient painter Polygnotos of Thassos who lived in the first half of the 5th century B.C. i.e. the period in which the Lesche was built. The subjects of these paintings were *the Destruction of Troy* and *the Descent of Ulysses to Hades*. Other famous paintings by Polygnotos were in the Poikile Stoa of Athens.

The very detailed description of Polygnotos's paintings by Pausanias in conjunction with contemporary vase paintings make it possible to recapture the essence of these paintings today. From ancient literary sources it is known that Polygnotos had brought a renewal into the art of painting by representing people in postures which expressed their mental states.

The Stadium

An ascending path leads from the theatre to the stadium. On the way, there is an ancient fountain known by its modern name: Kerna. In the rocks flanking the path, one can see recesses which contained various offerings – statuettes and the like.

The stadium was built in the 5th century B.C. as attested by an inscription on the southern retaining wall which forbids visitors to carry wine out of the stadium and mentions the fine imposed on transgressors. In the early periods, the spectators sat on the ground. Much later, Herodes Atticus paid for rows of seats to be built of Parnassus stone – and not of white marble as mentioned by Pausanias. At the entrance, four pillars (the two in the middle with recesses for statues) formed three arches, through which the athletes and the judges of the games entered the stadium (Pl. 54).

The stadium is 177.55 m. in length (1 stadium of the Roman era) and 25.50 m. on the average in width. The beginning and the end of the track are marked by two rows of slabs – the *start* and *finish* – with notches to provide a hold for the feet of the runners and rectangular holes into which were put the posts that separated the athletes.

The track is surrounded by the rows of seats; that part of the stadium was called the *theatre* and it consists of two long sides coming together in a semicircle – the *sphendone* – at one end. The rows of seats do not reach down to the track but end at a high wall – the podium – which is 1.30 m. high.

At the uppermost part of the stadium, there is a narrow gangway running around the periphery to facilitate the movement of the spectators. This gangway could be reached from the outside by two staircases situated at the eastern ends of the long sides of the stadium; also allowing access to the gangway were two very steep flights of stairs, one at the eastern end of the northern tiers, the other at the southern tiers where the semicircle of the sphendone begins. On the northern side there are 12 tiers, on the southern side only 6, as a result of the sloping ground. The tiers are interrupted by flights of stairs also to facilitate circulation within the stadium. In the middle of the northern side, there is a lengthy bench provided with back-rest and taking up the width of two rows of seats. These were the seats of honour for the judges.

At the northwestern end of the peripheral gangway there is a vaulted structure which served to protect a fountain used by the spectators.

The Games

The Pythian Games dedicated to Apollo were an event of panhellenic significance, commemorating the killing of the monster Python who guarded the ancient sanctuary of Earth, by Apollo. In the beginning the games were held every 8 years, but after the first

Sacred War this interval was shortened to 4 years. The first official games were celebrated in 582 B.C. The tyrant of Sicyon Cleisthenes won the chariot races on that occasion and it seems probable that his chariot, which he dedicated to Apollo, was kept in the monopteral treasury of Sicyon (see p. 14).

The new games, unlike the old, were not only musical but also gymnic (athletic) and equestrian. The festivities began on the 6th day of the month Boucatius (August-September). On the 9th, the musical competitions were held and on the 10th the athletic events took place including: stadium foot race, double-stadium race (diaulos), long-distance race (dolichos), wrestling, boxing and pancratium. On the 11th, the equestrian competitions were held in the plain of Krissa, and these, as the ancient poets inform us, were the most splendid part of the games.

Before the stadium was built, the games were held in the plain of Krissa where the hippodrome was located. From the second part of the 5th century onwards, they were held in the stadium, and the festivities included dramatic performances. From an inscription referring to the gymnasium and dating from 330–325 B.C., we are informed that a wooden stage would be set up for such occasions. Another inscription found in front of the portico of the Athenians and dating from the 2nd century B.C., says about the flute-player Satyros, son of Eumenes of Samos: *he was the first to play the flute alone, without competitors, at the games, and to present to the god and to the Greeks after the gymnic competitions on the occasion of the sacrifice to the Pythian god, at the stadium, a choric song with the title Dionysus and a piece from Euripides' «Bacchae» with guitar accompaniment.*

The Castalia Spring

The water of the sacred Castalia spring rises to the surface from the rock of Yambia in the wild ravine formed by the two Phedriads. Nowhere better than here do we see the char-

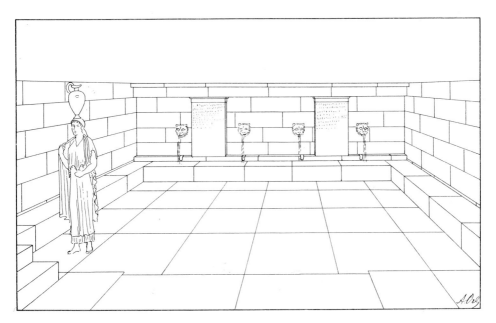

The Castalia in the archaic period (Reconstruction by A. K. Orlandos).

acteristic tendency of the Greeks to improve upon nature. They hewed the hard rock from which the water sprang into a rectangular space with 8 steps descending into it (Pl. 55).

The perpendicular surface of the rock at the far end was covered with stone slabs to a height of 2.50 m. The water ran out of the mouths of 7 bronze lion heads attached to this wall. Recesses hewn into the upper levels of the rock were used to place offerings, statuettes, cookies.

The structures seen at present date from the Hellenistic and Roman periods. In the archaic and classical eras, the water of the Castalia spring probably came out at a lower level, through a fountain whose ruins can be seen beside the road. This structure, excavated only a few years ago, was – in its last form at least – a paved courtyard with benches along three walls. The northern wall was fitted with four bronze lion heads whose muzzles served as outlets for the water.

Pindar's paean referring to the water of the spring and to the bronze lion heads from which it flowed, probably alluded to this latter fountain which seems to be older that the one hewn out of the Castalia rock.

The water of the Castalia spring was an important element in the worship of Apollo and the function of the oracle. From Euripides *(Ion)* we know that the temple of Apollo was sprinkled with this water, and that the priests and other officials of the temple as well as the pilgrims visiting the sanctuary went to Castalia to cleanse themselves. In subsequent years, the idea seems to have taken hold, that the water of the Castalia conferred prophetic and poetic powers.

The Sanctuary of Athene Pronaia

Proceeding from the Castalia along the public highway in the direction of Arachova, we meet the path leading through an olive-covered area to the sanctuary of Athene Pronaia (Marmaria). The name *Pronaia* (*pro* = before + *naos* = temple) is due to the fact that persons coming to Delphi from the east (eastern Sterea Hellas) met this sanctuary before coming to the temple of Apollo, which was the important temple of Delphi. The entrance to the sanctuary of Athene Pronaia was on the eastern side, while another gate at the western end of the sanctuary led to the gymnasium.

The beginnings of the sanctuary go back to the Mycenaean period. The excavation of the place of the altars and under the ancient temple of Athene showed that a female deity, a precursor of Athene, was worshipped here as attested by the female clay figurines now in the museum (see p. 4 and 44).

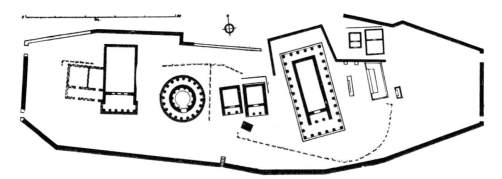

Topographical plan of the sanctuary of Athene Pronaia (P. de La Coste - Messelière).

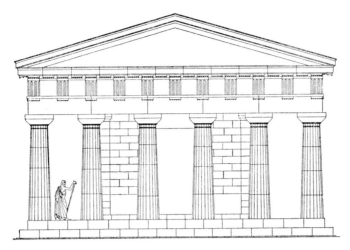

The porous stone temple of Athene Pronaia (Reconstruction by R. Demangel).

Upon entering the sanctuary, one first encounters the altars: there is a large one in the middle and a number of smaller altars, all masonry, around it. The altars leaning on the northern retaining wall are accompanied by inscriptions engraved on that wall: EILEITHIA on the right, HYGIEIA on the left. Three column-altars standing more to the fore are also identified by inscriptions as being dedicated to ZEUS POLIEUS the one, ATHENA FARGANAI the second, and ATHENA ZOSTERIAI the third. The attributes of the goddess are characteristic: one signifies the Athene who gives knowledge and prosperity, the other the Athene who helps women in childbirth and protects the health of men.

On the plateau formed by the wall bearing the inscriptions identifying the altars, there are two small temple-like structures, probably parts of the shrine of the local hero Phylacus. When the Persians attacked Delphi in 480 B.C., Phylacus, a giant, came forward with another hero called Autonoos and put them to flight.

The porous stone temple of Athene Pronaia stood next to the altars. The original temple built on this spot, also of porous stone, dated back to the middle of the 7th century B.C., and was one of the earliest important temples in Greece. We know of its existence from a few preserved parts of its columns and from 12 capitals which are interesting as specimens of an art advanced ahead of its time; they look like loaves of leavened, then compressed, bread.

This 7th-century-temple was destroyed and to replace it, a new temple of Athene was erected in 500 B.C. The new temple was also of porous stone, of the Doric order, peripteral with 6 columns along the short sides and 12 columns along the long sides. It had a pronaos with two columns, and a long nave, but had no *opisthodomos* (rear chamber). As the place was continuously endangered by the instability of the soil and the rocks that fell from the Phedriads, and as the building began to show damage, an attempt was made to consolidate it by filling with masonry the intervals between the columns at the northeastern corner, as can be seen from the ruins. When the temple was excavated, it had 15 columns standing intact, but in March 1905 abundant rains caused a fall of rocks (still lying about among the ruins) from Yambia and completed its destruction.

Croesus, king of Lydia, had dedicated a large gold shield to the 7th-century-temple of Athene and this, according to Herodotus, was later moved to the new temple. During the Third Sacred War, the Phocians removed the shield along with other valuable offerings in order to meet the expenses of the war.

To the west of the porous stone temple, there are the ruins of two treasuries made of Paros marble; one is of the Doric order, built after the Persian Wars around 480–470 B.C., with two columns between two door-posts in the front, the other is smaller in size, of the Ionic order, and built around 530 B.C. by the citizens of Massilia (Marseilles). The two columns in the front of the latter temple had capitals of the so-called Aeolic type: palm leaves bent downwards surround these capitals (see p. 37). This treasury is one of the loveliest buildings in Delphi and can only be compared with the treasury of Siphnos for artistic beauty. On the outside, there was a frieze, of which a few pieces have been preserved, along the upper part of the walls. In later years, the Romans placed in this treasury statues of their emperors; the statues stood on the long base which extends across the whole width of the building.

The treasury of Massilia
(Reconstruction by W. B. Dinsmoor).

The stones with deep grooves seen around both treasuries served to fasten slabs bearing inscriptions.

In front of the two treasuries there is a large stone pedestal in a slightly oblique position. There is good reason to believe that this was the base of the trophy erected by Delphi – according to the historian Diodorus – at the sanctuary of the Pronaia as an offering to Zeus and Apollo for their help, in the form of a fall of rocks, in driving away the Persians when the latter were besieging Delphi in 480 B.C. Next to the base of this trophy there is another small pedestal on which stood a statue of the Roman Emperor Hadrian, erected in 125 A.D. by the priest of Apollo pursuant to a decision of the Amphictyonic Council. This information is provided by an inscription on the face of the pedestal. The same priest – Titus Flavius Aristotimus – had been instrumental in erecting at the sanctuary of Apollo the statue of Antinoos which will be seen in the museum.

The round structure to the west of the treasuries is the Tholos, a masterpiece of ancient architecture built around 380 B.C. Theodorus Phocaeus who was, perhaps, the architect, had written a book on this building according to Vitruvius's information (Pl. 58).

The Tholos is of Doric order and had on the outside 20 columns supporting an entablature (epistyle, triglyphs, metopes with reliefs, a cornice). The circular wall corresponding to the nave of the temple on the outside was also ornamented with triglyphs and metopes with reliefs, while 10 Corinthian semicolumns (engaged col.) were attached to the inside surface of the wall of the nave (see Room of the Tholos in the museum). What the exact purpose of the Tholos was is uncertain, but the lavishness with which it was built, its multicoloured materials (Pentelic marble and dark limestone from Eleusis), the delicacy of the work (the cyma with leaves in relief at the foot of the wall of the nave is exquisite) indicate that it had some special significance and, in any case, make it one of the most beautiful buildings of antiquity.

The great earthquake of 373 B.C. which destroyed many buildings in Delphi and in particular the temple of Apollo (the one built by the Alcmeonidae) apparently caused damage so severe to the second porous stone temple of Athene that it had to be abandoned as dangerous. Though ruined, the temple was still in the sanctuary at the time of Pausanias.

The new temple of Athene was built of grey stone from Prophitis Ilias (a stone quarry near Delphi) west of the Tholos in 370 B.C. approximately. Its plan was simpler than that of the previous porous stone structure: Doric order with 6 columns in the front only and with some peculiarities in the design. The pronaos was broader than the nave and there were two Ionic semicolumns between two door-posts of the same order on the wall separating the pronaos from the nave. The metopes were unadorned.

It should be noted, however, that the perfection of the stonework and the mathematical austerity in the conception and the execution of the design make of the stone temple of Athene one of the most attractive and most interesting monuments of Delphi.

The last structure before crossing the western gate toward the gymnasium is the one adjacent to the western side of the stone temple of Athene, the so-called «house of priests», including a *prodomos* and two rooms at the back. It is an older construction than the temple.

The Tholos of the sanctuary of Athene Pronaia (Reconstruction by H. Pomtow).

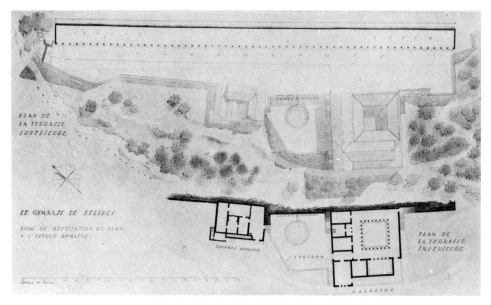

Plan of the gymnasium of Delphi (J. Jannoray).

The Gymnasium

At the foot of one of the Phedriads, the Yambia, halfway between the sanctuary of Athene Pronaia and the Castalia spring, below the public highway, there are the ruins of the gymnasium of Delphi. According to the legend, the area of the *paradromis* (track for running excercices) was covered in very ancient times by a thick forest. While hunting in this forest with the sons of Autolycus, Ulysses had been wounded at the leg by a boar. It was from the scar of this wound that his faithful maid-servant Eurycleia knew Ulysses when he returned to Ithaca ten years after the Trojan War.

The group of buildings of the gymnasium served for the training of the youths of Delphi and for the preparation of the athletes participating in the Pythian Games. But from the Hellenistic period onwards, the uses and purposes of the gymnasium became considerably broader. Foreign teachers, orators, poets and scientists came to Delphi and lectured at the gymnasium; various inscriptions tell about some of them: a grammarian from Acarnania, a Roman orator, an epic poet from Skepse, a Roman astronomer. We also know from an inscription that the torch-light procession during the Eumenian Games started from the gymnasium and ended at the altar of Apollo.

The gymnasium is built on two levels. The upper level included the *xystos* and the *paradromis* for running exercices, and the lower level included the *palaestra*, the *pool* for cold baths and the *thermae* for hot baths.

The palaestra consists of a square courtyard with an Ionic order peristyle, on two sides of which (N and W) there were several rooms. In the courtyard (the peristyle referred to in the inscriptions) boxing was practised, while the rooms around it served various other purposes, also known from inscriptions. The *apodyterion* (dressing-room), a main part of every palaestra, was perhaps the large room on the western side. There the athletes left their clothes or exercised in the nude. Another room, perhaps the first or third on the northern side, was the *konima* or *konisterion* i.e. the store-room for fine sand with which the athletes used to cover their bodies, and a third room was the *spheristerion*, in which boxers and pancratiasts, like their modern counterparts, trained with sand-filled bags. Between these two spaces there was, perhaps, the *ephebaeon* or *exedra*, a small temple-like building (two columns between door-posts a vestibule and at the back of the main room, perhaps, the statue of a deity of the gymnasium e.g. Hermes or Hercules).

Over the peristyle of the palaestra, a church dedicated to St. Mary was built in modern times, and on one of its columns – originally a column of the ancient gymnasium – Lord Byron and his friend Hobhouse scratched their names in 1809.

A passageway led from the palaestra to the *bath*. This consisted mainly of a round pool approximately in the middle of a spacious courtyard, and of 10 stone basins in two groups, leaning on the strong retaining wall of the northeastern side. The basins were placed side-by-side and received water from 11 openings in the wall overhead. The openings were fitted with bronze heads of animals, probably lions. There was an appropriate conduit through which the water from the basins (these communicated with one another) and from the central lion head flowed into the round pool where the athletes bathed after exercise.

Through the Roman conquest, new customs were imported into Greece. These included public hot baths, and such facilities (thermae) began to appear, at first for the sake of the Romans, in many places, and in particular at the gymnasia. Delphi did not fail to comply with the new vogue and thermae were constructed outside the sanctuary of Apollo, in the large portico west of the offering of Crateros and within its recess. Other thermae were built to the south of the *Stoa* of Attalos, the latter, as mentioned earlier, serving as a water reservoir. At the gymnasium the thermae were west of the round pool. They consisted of a rectangular structure which was made up of two large rooms – one on the northern and one on the southern side – with three smaller rooms between them. The floor of these rooms, with the exception of the large southern hall, rested on short clay supports leaving a hollow space through which hot air circulated *(hypocaust)*.

The upper terrace of the gymnasium was used for race training. It included a large portico (called *xystos* = scraped, because the floor had always to be perfectly levelled out and compacted); in the front there was a colonnade which in the early years was of the Doric order and made of porous stone, while in Roman times it was of the Ionic order and made of marble. The distance between *start* and *finish* was 184.830 m., i.e. the length of a Delphic stadium. The *xystos* was used for running practice when the weather was hot or otherwise inclement; the uncovered track in front of the *xystos*, known as *paradromis* served the same purpose in fine weather.

THE MUSEUM

I. Vestibule: The sculptured marble block facing the visitor mounting the steps to the museum is a copy of the famous Delphi «umbilicus» (*omphalos*) which was kept in the adyton of the temple. It was the symbol of the god, of the sanctuary, and of Delphi in general. According to the legend, Zeus had once decided to find the centre of the world and for this purpose had let two eagles loose at the outermost points of the universe.

The delphic omphalos.

Flying towards each other, the birds had met over Delphi, thus indicating that this was the centre of the earth, the navel of the world. The umbilicus is covered by a network of woollen bands, the *agrenon*. Two gilted eagles stood on top of it or at its sides. According to tradition, the umbilicus was the grave of the dragon Python, son of the goddess Earth and guardian of her oracle, whom Apollo had slain before taking possession of the oracle.

The small relief of Pentelic marble (probably the work of some Athenian workshop) to the left of the umbilicus, representing Athene, the umbilicus and Apollo, is the upper part of a stele which bore an inscription – a decree honouring Demades, one of the ten greatest Athenian orators – and dates from about 330 B.C.

The lengthy white marble relief in the narrow passageway of the vestibule is what remains of the frieze of the proscenium of the Delphic theatre – a sample of provincial classicism of the 1st century A.D. The slim and tall figures are impressive, and the scenes depicted from left to right are: Hercules in the Garden of the Hesperides; Cerberus; Hercules and the Nemean Lion; Hercules fighting Centaur; Hercules fighting the Hydra of Lerna; Hercules with Antaeus; an Amazon fighting scene; Hercules wearing his characteristic lion skin cloak; the three-bodied Geryon; Hercules fighting the son of Mars (Ares) Diomedes and one of his carnivore horses; Hercules shooting at the Birds of Stymphalus with his arrow.

II. The Room of the Shields: Most exhibits in this room date from the 7th century B.C., for example, the three bronze shields (first half of the 7th century) one of which has a decorative design of concentric circles interrupted by acute angles, while the other two have a lioness head in the middle, surrounded by other animals: rams, and deer and lions respectively.

The small Ionic column of Paros marble supported, according to the inscription engraved on it, an offering by the sons of Charopinus who was possibly a sculptor from Paros (middle of 6th century B.C.), while the bronze statuette representing a young man and dedicated to Apollo (a Cretan work of the second half of the 7th century B.C.) is a characteristic example of the so-called «Deadalic» art (Pl. 65). The wrought bronze griffin (7th century B.C.) is part of the decoration of the bronze cauldron which together with the tripod was the most typical offering to Apollo.

The last exhibit in this room is a Paros marble (now partly restored with plaster) sprinkler (*perirranterion*): three girls around a column supported a marble basin. The bronze cauldron does not belong to this group (early 6th century B.C.).

III. The Room of the Kouroi: The two large Paros marble archaic statues represent, according to a hypothesis put forward by the first experts who studied them, two brothers from Argos named Cleovis and Biton. As Herodotus tells the story, their mother was a priestess of Hera and one festive day, when she absolutely had to go to the sanctuary of the goddess and the oxen which were to pull her carriage failed to come, the two young men yoked themselves to the carriage and took her there in time. Pleased with the behaviour of her sons and by the flattering comments of the Argives assembled at the sanctuary, the mother begged the goddess to reward the boys. After the feast, the boys went to sleep in the sanctuary and died peacefully in their sleep. To honour them, the Argives dedicated their statues (the work of the Argive sculptor *[Poly]medes*) to Apollo. They date from 610–580 B.C., and are an example of the transition from the «Daedalic» style of the 7th century to the archaic style of the 6th century B.C. The characteristic features of this art are a sense of volume, firm and wellshaped bodies conveying an impression of athletic vigour, wide-open eyes lending the faces an air of aliveness (Pl. 66).

The five metopes (they were 14 in number originally) made of porous stone from Sicyon, whose pale whitish hue contrasted sharply with the deep-red colour of the garments worn by the figures, come from the treasury of Sicyon known as *monopteral* (see p. 14), and are exquisite examples of the archaic art of Sicyon around the middle of the 6th century (560 B.C.) – an art greatly admired in antiquity.

The linear element is the main feature of the art of these small pictures, where contours and details stand out as though they were parts of a drawing. They represent from left to right: (a) an incident from the expedition of the Argonauts, an extremely unusual subject in the archaic period. In the foreground are the Dioscuri Castor and Pollux depicted as horsemen, and in the background, towards the middle, the front part of the ship Argo and standing in it Orpheus and a musician playing the lyre in an effort to appease the furious waves; (b) Europa, the Phoenician princess, being carried off by Zeus in the form of a bull; bent forward on the animal's back, Europa holds onto the running bull; (c) the Dioscuri Castor and Pollux armed with spears and their cousins Idas and Lyngeus, sons of Apharides, abducting oxen. Coloured inscriptions identify the figures in this unique plastic representation of this episode from the myth of the Dioscuri; (d) a phase in the hunt of the Calydonian Boar showing the terrible wild beast that devastated Aetolia (Pl. 67). The hunt, in which took part all the heroes of the subsequent Expedition of the Argonauts, was organised by Meleager, son of Oeneus, king of Calydon, and it was Meleager himself who in the end killed the boar; under the boar can be seen the remains of one of Meleager's dogs attacking the beast; (e) a scene from the myth of the Golden Fleece. The destroyed metope depicted the mythical Phrixus riding the ram with the golden fleece.

The small bronze statue representing a young man or Apollo with a necklace is an important work of ancient plastic art (530–520 B.C. approximately) and bears certain similarities with Laconic or Ionic works of the same kind (Pl. 65).

IV. The Room of Siphnos: The large room commonly known as the «Room of Siphnos» includes some fine specimens of the mature archaic art of ancient Greece and in particular the remains of the reliefs of the frieze of the treasury of Siphnos, which dates from 525 B.C. (see p. 14).

The sculptural decorations of the treasury, made of Paros marble and painted with bright colours at some places, are believed to be the work of two groups of craftsmen, each under a sculptor with his assistant, whose names have not been preserved.

The western and southern frieze are made by the one sculptor and his group, and show tendencies reminiscent of Ionic art. It would seem that their maker had lived or worked in one of the great artistic centres of the coast of Asia Minor, such as Erythrae, Smyrna, Phocaea, Colophon. His art, self-contained, static, is akin to painting.

The other artist, the younger of the two, who made the northern and the eastern frieze, seems to have been exposed to the influence of the art of Chios or one of the other islands off the coast of Asia Minor. His art is plastic, narrative, and bears the mark of the artistic activity of Attica to a greater extent than the art of the other sculptor.

Eastern Frieze: This part of the frieze, whose subject is the Trojan War, is divided into two sections, like a diptych. The first part of the left-hand section shows a council of the gods watching from Olympus the battle taking place outside the walls of Troja and depicted in the right-hand section of the frieze. The gods are divided into two groups, the protectors of the Trojans and the Greeks, respectively. On the left are shown the gods favouring the Trojans turned towards their protegés – an indication of their favour. First, there is Ares wearing his armour as befits the god of war, sitting at one end. Next to him Aphrodite (or Leto), Artemis, Apollo turned towards his sister, and finally Zeus in a magnificent throne decorated with a relief showing a Silenus chasing a nymph. In front of Zeus there was Thetis, Achilles's mother, as a suppliant (parts of her fingers touching the knees of Zeus in supplication are preserved). A little further and turned to the left, like the Greeks, were the gods favouring them: Poseidon, of whom nothing remains, Athene, Hera and Demeter. The scene depicts a well-known episode of the Trojan War: Zeus, implored by Thetis, temporarily turned against the Greeks, until the injustice done to her son Achilles by Agamemnon in taking from him the girl Briseis had been restored (Pl. 68).

In the second section, the battle going on outside the walls of Troy is shown. On the left are the Trojans: first a Trojan four-horse chariot with the charioteer Glaucus, then Aenaeas and Hector. On the right are the Greeks: Menelaus holding a shield decorated with a Gorgon head, Ajax, a Greek four-horse chariot with the charioteer Automedon and finally, alone at the end, Nestor the wise adviser of the Greeks, urging them by his attitude to the action that will bring them victory. On the ground a dead warrior (Pl. 69).

Northern Frieze: This frieze depicts the war between the Olympian gods and the Giants. At the left end, Hephaestus in his blacksmith's shop filling his furnace bags with air, while in front of him two goddesses are fighting with two giants. Further ahead the goddess Cybele (behind her Hercules or Dionysus at grips with a giant) in a chariot drawn by two lions which are tearing a giant to pieces. In front of her, Apollo and Artemis (at their feet the giant Ephialtas is already dead and a little farther right the giant Astartas is just falling) are shooting with their arrows at three shielded giants and the giant Cantharus flees in terror from Cybele's lions. Further on Zeus (not preserved) on his chariot is attacked by two giants. In the foreground, Hera bends to finish off a fallen giant; on her right, Athene has stricken down Verectas and is fighting with Laertas while Astartas is dying. A little further Ares is struggling with Viatas and Enafas, one of whom is picking up a stone to throw at the god. Immediately after, Hermes with raised sword is attacking two giants. On their right, part of Poseidon's body is preserved. At the extremity of the frieze, an unidentified god is fighting with two giants (Pl. 70).

As the northern side of the treasury looked upon the Sacred Way, the ascending pilgrims would admire the uniform unfolding of the action from left to right and the narrative power of the artist, who has remained anonymous though he tried to immortalize his name in a sentence engraved on the shield of the third giant being shot at by Apollo and Artemis; it is precisely the part of the sentence containing the artist's name that has not been preserved.

Western Frieze: This frieze told the story of the «Judgment of Paris». Eris, the goddess of discord, not having been invited to the wedding of Peleus and Thetis for obvious reasons, revenged the insult by throwing among the guests an apple inscribed: «For the most beautiful». This caused a quarrel between Aphrodite, Athene and Hera who each claimed the prize, and to end the strife, Zeus asked Paris, the young prince of Troy, to decide. Paris awarded the apple to Aphrodite.

In the frieze, which unrolls in the way of a triptych, Hermes is shown at the left-hand end as a charioteer in the winged four-horse chariot of Athene who, winged herself, is hurriedly getting on the carriage. The male figure behind her is Hephaestus or Poseidon. Next the victorious Aphrodite is shown, getting off her chariot while trying to put a necklace around her neck (Pl. 71). The admirable ingenuity and originality of the artist in presenting his theme and working out the details will be found again in the southern frieze. Though severely damaged, Aphrodite is still one of the loveliest figures in the whole sculptural decoration of the treasury of Siphnos. The right-hand part of the frieze has not been preserved, but it can be assumed with certainty that it included a third chariot, and Hera.

Southern Frieze: It is difficult to decide on the meaning of the southern frieze or on the correct sequence of its preserved parts. Likely themes are the abduction of the daughters of Leucippus, king of Messenia, by the Dioscuri Castor and Pollux, or Hippodamia, daughter of the king of Elis Oenomaos, being carried off by Pelops, with Oenomaos starting to chase them.

The parts preserved show first an abduction scene, and on the left a woman going away. In the middle, there is an altar with a four-horse chariot in front of it (Pl. 71), and finally two young horsemen followed by another four-horse chariot. The movement, the postures and the shapes of the horses are admirably depicted and are unique from this point of view in the archaic art of the Greeks.

Of the two pediments of the treasury of Siphnos, only the eastern i.e. the one of the rear side of the building has been preserved. It is made of Paros marble and is displayed in the museum above the corresponding frieze. Its theme is purely Delphic: the quarrel between Apollo and Hercules about the possession of the prophetic tripod. When Pythia refused to give Hercules an answer because he had not yet atoned for the murder of Iphitus, Hercules carried off the tripod with the intention to establish an oracle of his own. In the middle of the scene, there is Artemis holding back the furious Apollo who wants to snatch the tripod from Hercules, the latter having shouldered the tripod and moving away. Standing between the two and trying to appease them is Athene (or Zeus) (Pl. 67).

High up on the far wall, beside the Battle of the Giants, two pieces of the drain pipe of the treasury of Siphnos are displayed. The one on the left is decorated with reliefs (anthemions, lotus), the one on the right has in addition a lion head in the middle, serving as a waterspout for the water dripping from the roof.

The female statue made of Paros marble to the left of the Sphinx of Naxos is one of the two Caryatids used instead of columns in the front of the treasury (Pl. 72). It is an example of the richness of the treasury, as this statue was in antiquity adorned with a multitude of inlaid gems, as can be seen from the holes drilled through its hair, at the site of the diadem, and at the ears. On the girl's lips, one sees the characteristic archaic smile. The *calathos* or *polos* she carries on her head is decorated with a representation of a maenad or nymph moving away on the right, a Silenus seizing a maenad while he dances and the remains of another Silenus, on the left. The calathos supported the bell-shaped capital exhibited on a high pedestal to the left of the Caryatid. On the echinus of this capital there is a relief showing two lions devouring a deer. This Caryatid is believed to be the work of the sculptor who made the eastern and the northern frieze of the treasury of Siphnos, while the reliefs of the calathos and the capital are attributed to the artist of the southern and the western frieze.

To the left of the capital of this Caryatid can be seen the remains of another female statue dressed in a *chiton* under a short *himation*. The right hand of the girl holds the chiton which forms folds indicated by engraved lines. The folds start from the right hand of the girl, spread out radially around the body and come back to the hand. The style is reminiscent of the archaic art of Samos and of eastern Greece in general. The prevailing opinion is that this statue served as a Caryatid at the treasury of Cnidos, but this is not certain. It dates from the middle of the 6th century B.C., approximately.

Some members of the *perithyron* (doorway decoration) of the treasury of Siphnos are displayed behind the Caryatid of the same treasury. Here again the sumptuousness that characterised the building is seen in the rich decoration with floral reliefs (anthemions, lotus, rosettes) and in the overall design of this piece which is reminiscent of its counterpart in the Erechtheion of the Acropolis of Athens.

The pieces displayed on the right of the *perithyron* of the treasury of Siphnos are parts of a structure which probably housed some valuable offering or cult object in the archaic temple of Apollo. The faces of the structure were decorated with reliefs (Ionic cyma, astragal, anthemions and lotus – Last quarter of the 6th century B.C.).

The remains of feet and the base with inscription exhibited opposite the headless female statue described above, belonged to the image of a young man which, like the small column in the room of the shields, was dedicated by the sons of Charopinus, probably a sculptor from Paros (middle of 6th century B.C.). The Aeolic capital seen to the right of the feet of this offering comes from the treasury of Massilia in the sanctuary of Athene Pronaia (530-510 B.C.).

The Paros marble head (approx. 525 B.C.) to the right of the Sphinx of Naxos belonged to a Caryatid of an unidentified treasury (according to recent research findings, it may be the head of the second Caryatid of the treasury of Siphnos; it was formerly believed to come from the treasury of Cnidos). The eyes were of inlaid glass. The head, elaborately worked, bore the type of diadem known as «crown», and was richly decorated. The *polos* shows a representation of Apollo the Guitar-Player, followed by four nymphs. In front of Apollo, to the right, three Graces and Hermes playing the flute (Pl. 73).

The Sphinx (Naxos marble, 570-560 B.C.), an offering of the citizens of Naxos to Apollo, is one of the largest plastic works found at Delphi and a representative sample of archaic Naxian art. It stood on the Ionic capital of a column with 44 flutings and 6 drums which was retained by a rock in front of the great polygonal wall of the sanctuary of Apollo west of the Stoa of the Athenians. The offering rose to a total height of approximately 12.10 m. (12.45 m. to the tips of the wings) and the drum of the base was inscribed with a decree renewing the Naxians' right of precedence in receiving oracles (*promanteia*) (328-327 B.C.).

The Sphinx presents the characteristic features of Naxian art – an art which, associated with the political supremacy of Naxos in the Cyclades, exercised considerable influence from the late 7th century and throughout the 6th century B.C. There are linear and graphic elements in the shaping of the hair, the chest and the wings of the Sphinx. The monument stood perhaps, at the extremity of the ancient sanctuary of Earth (see p. 16) where Apollo had slain Python, as a guardian of the oracle or as a symbol of Naxos. The face of the Sphinx bears a dreamy, quizzical expression enlivened by the archaic smile on her lips (Pl. 74).

The two small Doric columns behind the Sphinx belonged to a monument dating from the 6th century B.C.

V. The Room of the Treasury of Athens: The 24 metopes contained in this room, all of Paros marble, are the main elements of the sculptural decoration of the treasury of Athens (490-489 B.C.), which now stands restored in the sanctuary of Apollo. They represent the battle between the Athenians and the Amazons (mythical female warriors of Asia), the feats of Theseus, the national hero of Athens, and the Attic-Delphic version of the Labours of Hercules.

Five or six of the best artists of Athens worked at the making of the 30 metopes which originally adorned the building. Two styles can be distinguished in the rendering of the figures, the presentation of the scenes and the work of the details: one rather conservative and archaic, the other more modern and classical. A representative example of the former style is the metope showing Hercules and the Hind of Ceryneia, and examples of the latter style are the metopes representing Theseus with the Minotaur and Hercules with Cycnus.

On either side of the entrance to the room are displayed those metopes that have been preserved out of the nine decorating the northern side of the treasury and representing the

Labours of Hercules. Leaving out the two extreme metopes, which show warriors and are not certainly connected with the Labours, the others represent in a right-to-left order: Hercules fighting with and overcoming the Centaur; Hercules about to finish off the already wounded terrible robber Cycnus (Pl. 75); Hercules jumping and seizing the Hind of Ceryneia by the head (Pl. 76; noteworthy is the accurate and detailed anatomy of the hero's body) and finally one of the best-known Labours – Hercules standing in struggle with the Nemean Lion; the hero has lifted the monster and is about to suffocate it.

Of the six remaining metopes, to the left of those already discussed, five depict the tenth labour, namely the fight of Hercules with Geryon, a three-bodied monster first described by Hesiod, and the abduction of his herds by Hercules. Geryon, mythical grandson of Medusa, kept the oxen of *Helios* (Sun) in Erythia, a legendary country at the westernmost confines of the earth. The metopes depict the herds of Geryon, oxen and cows, the three-bodied giant himself as a warrior, and his dog Orthros in the thralls of death.

The six metopes opposite the Labours of Hercules, and the last metope on the side of the Geryon series, adorned the southern side of the treasury. They were so placed as to catch the light and so were visible from afar. They told of the exploits of Theseus, the legendary king of Attica who unified the tribes of the area and made Athens his capital.

Seen from right to left, they represent: Theseus charging against a fallen robber, perhaps Procrustes, then Theseus at grips with the robber Cercyon, the hero holding the robber by the waist and trying to lift him off the ground, Theseus again (not preserved) fighting with another robber, perhaps Sciron who is fallen upon a rock, and finally the hero standing in a worshipful attitude before Athene who wears a chiton, a himation and an aegis, and grants him her divine protection.

Beyond the doorway, the remaining three metopes show Theseus overcoming the Bull of Marathon, who crumples to the ground, then preparing to kill the Queen of the Amazons Antiope (Pl. 75), with whom he fell in love and had a son, Hippolytus. The last metope on this side shows Theseus at his best-known exploit, the slaying of the Minotaur, the monster with the body of a man and the head of a bull who devoured the seven boys and seven girls sent every nine years by the Athenians as a levy to Minos, king of Crete. In this representation, Theseus has seized the Minotaur by the head and is about to strike him.

The six metopes across the room from those showing Hercules steeling the oxen of Geryon, adorned the façade of the treasury. They depict the war the Athenians fought against the Amazons and symbolise the triumph of the Greek spirit over obscure, irrational power.

In all the metopes of the treasury there is a harmonious and balanced combination of archaic and classical elements resulting in a unique sculptural decoration, a most exquisite expression of the simplicity and the freshness of Attic art during this period.

Above the metopes representing the Amazon War and the fight with Geryon, there are some fragments of sculptures from the pediments of the treasury. The eastern pediment depicted a peaceful scene, perhaps a meeting of two heros – Theseus and his friend Peirithous, king of the Lapiths, according to one hypothesis – before a deity; the western pediment represented a battle scene, the central figures being Hercules and Telamon fighting against Laomedon, king of Troy and father of Priam.

VI. First Room of the Temple of Apollo: The remains of the western pediment of the temple of Apollo (built towards 510 B.C. by the Alcmeonidae as contractors) occupy the whole length of one side of the room. The subject of this pediment was the battle between the gods of Olympus and the Giants. The material was Peloponnesian poros covered with stucco lustre on which the details of the figures were painted in colour. The Athenian sculptor Antenor is believed to be the author of this pediment. The monumental character of the figures, their earnest and austere magnificence are admirable and in perfect keeping with the dynamic stability of the Doric order. On the other hand, the movement that made the figures of this pediment look alive, contrasted with the majestic immobility of the statues of the eastern pediment.

At the left-hand extremity there is a fallen giant (perhaps Engeladus), and on the right Athene rushing to battle, a male figure and the front parts of two horses.

Near the western pediment there is a small clothed image of a man, dating from the early 5th century B.C., and to its right a fine headless female Paros marble figure, wearing the *peplos*, walking hurriedly – perhaps a messenger of the gods. This statue possibly served as an acro terium in the Doric temple of Athene Pronaia (insular workshop, around 470 B.C.).

Opposite this female statue, a part of the southern wall of the treasury of Athens is displayed; it is engraved with two hymns to Apollo, with musical notes indicating the melody, between the lines. The author of these hymns was probably an Athenian poet, and it is likely that they were first sung to guitar and double-flute accompaniment at the Athenian Pythaids of 138 and 128 B.C. by the Athens 40 to 60-member community singing group known as the *Artists of Dionysus*. A *Pythais* was an official Athenian delegation in the form of a great religious procession sent by Athens to Delphi at certain intervals as a token of respect for the Pythian Apollo.

VII. Second Room of the Temple of Apollo: This room is dominated by the sculptural decoration of the eastern pediment (510 B.C.) of the archaic temple of Apollo. The Alcmeonidae who had been appointed contractors for the construction of this temple attempted, according to Herodotus, to gain favour with the sanctuary by using Paros marble instead of the porous stone foreseen by their contract, in the sculptural decoration of this pediment and in the eastern façade of the temple.

The theme of this pediment was the *Epiphany* of Apollo, i.e. his triumphal arrival at Delphi with his sister Artemis and his mother Leto. In the centre was the chariot with these deities and on either side of it, Delphus (right) the local king, welcoming Apollo, and the Athenian *Sons of Hephaestus* whose task was – as Aeschylus says in his «Eumenides» – to clear the way and tame the wild earth, and (left) three female statues, possibly Pandrosus, Erse and Aglaurus, the daughters of Cecrops. At the corners of the pediments there are groups of animals: on the left a lion killing a bull, on the right a lion tearing at a deer. Details of the statues, such as the wounds of the animals, were painted red (Pl. 76).

To the right of the pediment, there is a female statue – a winged Victory – which served as an apical acroterium in the archaic temple of Apollo (Pl. 77), a partly restored fragment of the drain pipes of the temple and a marble image of a young man, dating from around 555-540 B.C. To the left of the pediment, there is again a headless Sphinx, a lateral acroterium at the archaic temple of Apollo; a partly restored fragment of the drain pipes of the temple (4th century) (Pl. 78), and another marble image of a young man from the period 540-520 B.C.

The small bronze statue of a walking cow, an offering to Apollo, dates from the late 6th or early 5th century B.C., while the bronze statuettes of athletes (one holding dumb-bells in his left hand, the other a *stlengis* in his right) date from the first half of the 5th century B.C.

The four inscribed steles opposite the pediment date from 361–310 B.C., and contain accounts kept by the city of Delphi concerning the reconstruction of the temple of Apollo after its destruction in 373 B.C., a list of contributions by cities and private citizens also in connection with the reconstruction of the temple, and a list of payments made by the Phocians in respect of a levy imposed on them after their defeat in the Third Sacred War.

The large inscription over the door of the room refers to repair work done to the temple of Apollo with funds made available by the Emperor of Rome Domitian, and dates from 84 A.D.

VIII. The Room of Funerary Monuments: The main exhibit in this room is the fine Paros marble funerary stele of a young athlete, an example of early classical art (465 B.C., approx.), produced by some insular workshop.

The young man has just finished a wrestling exercice and is using a *stlengis* (a kind of scraper with a handle) to scrape off the dirt and the oil with which athletes used to salve their bodies. The slave child is holding a round bowl (*aryballus*) filled with aromatic oil, and between them, pointed muzzle upturned, the dead young man's dog. There is a marvelous harmony, a tenderness combined with solidity, in the design and the rendering of the figures (Pl. 78).

Across from the funerary monument just described, there are three others which, however, are less well preserved: a man wearing a heavy garment (late 6th century B.C.), a slave girl holding up a mirror to her mistress (middle 5th century B.C.) and a young naked slave carrying an aryballus as he accompanies his master to the palaestra (first half of 5th century B.C.). The vases exhibited in the small showcase at the wall were also found in graves (oil-flasks, amphora, alabaster containers, of the 5th century B.C.), two fine bronze pitchers on separate bases opposite (5th and 4th century B.C.) and three clay masks of Demeter or Persephone (5th century B.C.).

In the second part of the room, behind the funerary monument of the young man, there is a fine marble head representing Dionysus (Pl. 79); the grave of Dionysus was at Delphi and his worship was prevalent here. There is a dreamy, and gentle human expression on the handsome adolescent face, which is crowned with soft locks of hair. Around the forehead there is the characteristic band (miter) of the initiate (second half of 4th century B.C.).

To the right of the head of Dionysus stands a headless statue of Apollo the Guitar-Player, a common artistic subject of the period (early 3rd century B.C.), and at a corner, a round marble altar from the sanctuary of Athene Pronaia (Pl. 80), with a charming group of young girls hanging ribbons on a garland of leaves (middle of 1st century B.C.). On the wall above the altar, there is a representation of a head of a horse, which was probably part of a relief showing a four-horse chariot (late 5th century B.C.). The fine trunk of an athlete further to the right, as well as the two running female figures on either side of the doorway to the room of the Tholos belong to the 4th century B.C. The first (second half of 4th century B.C.) was possibly an acroterium in some building, the second was probably part of an offering (early 4th cent. B.C.).

IX. The Room of the Tholos: On the wall opposite the entrance there is a restored part of the entablature of the Tholos (see p. 28) i.e. the circular building in the sanctuary of Athene Pronaia (380–375 B.C.). The rich sculptural decoration shows a careful and neat craftsmanship down to the smallest detail (Pl. 58), and is made up of a number of metopes which are divided into two groups: the external or large metopes of island marble, which were placed over the 20 columns of the Doric peristyle; and the internal or small metopes made of Pentelic marble, which adorned the upper part of the wall of the nave. The themes of the representations appear to be the War of the Amazons and the War of the Centaurs (a war between Lapiths and Centaurs).

The art and style show clear Attic influence, in particular the influence of the sculptures of the Parthenon and the Erechtheion, and it is probable that the artists who made these metopes had learned their craft in Athenian workshops. The metopes exhibited here are the ones that are best preserved. The two extreme metopes were deliberately destroyed in the latest period of Antiquity.

The metopes, taken from left to right, represent: (a) a Centaur rising up on his hind legs after having seized a woman; (b) a rearing horse and another figure; (c) a Greek bending on his right knee trying to avoid a blow that an Amazon is about to strike; and (d) perhaps a man walking towards a column, behind which a woman can be seen.

The smaller sculptures exhibited along the two lateral walls of the room are parts of poorly preserved other metopes of the Tholos, and represent for the most part torsos of Amazons and Greek warriors; the three female torsos standing on separate bases, probably come from acroteria of various buildings and date from the first half of the 4th century B.C.

On either side of the doorway, there are a triglyph with its epistyle from the wall of the nave of the Tholos and one partly restored internal engaged column from the same building (left) and, upon a high pedestal, a Doric capital from the external colonnade of the Tholos (right).

X. The Room of Agias: One impressive exhibit in this room is the group of three young women of Pentelic marble who appear to be dancing on the tall floral column shaped in the form of a stylized sappy-looking stalk with indented, acanthus-like leaves (Pl. 59). Above the tall *calathos* they carried on their heads, there was a bronze cauldron resting on a tripod whose legs were fastened to the projecting thorns of the column.

The girls' legs seem to be moving in a slow, rhythmical dancing step; their left arms were raised while the left held an end of their short chitons which fall in multiple folds with an airy lightness and seem strangely real in the interplay of light and shadow around the vigorous young bodies. A fleeting smile lights up the earnest faces adorned with richly worked ear-rings.

The group stood originally in the sanctuary of Apollo, almost in front of the offering of Daochus, and had a total height of 13 m.; the column alone measured 11 m. and the girls' statues 2.08 m.

According to the inscription at the base, the group was an offering of the Athenians dating from the period 335-325 B.C. and the three girls are probably the daughters (Pandrosus, Erse and Aglaurus) of Cecrops, the legendary founder of Athens and father of the Attic tribes. We have already seen a representation of these daughters at the eastern pediment of the archaic temple of Apollo. A drum of the corresponding column is exhibited beside this group.

On the opposite side of the room, there are 6 statues, whose original bases we have seen in the sanctuary of Apollo (see p. 19). They are an offering of the Thessalian Daochus II from Pharsala. Daochus II, a well-known personality in his time, delegate (*hieromnemon*) of Thessaly to the Amphictyonic Council between 336 and 332 B.C. and president of the Amphictyonic Assembly at which he served the interests of Macedon, offered to Apollo around 335 B.C. a monument representing the most renowned members of his family (statesmen, warriors, victors at panhellenic athletic games). Seven generations of dead and living family members covering a period extending from the 6th century to 335 B.C., were presented together in an impressive family group consisting of 9 Paros marble statues (only six of them and the plinth of a 7th have been preserved). The names of the persons represented by these statues are known from the inscriptions – most of them in verse – engraved and still visible in the front ot the bases.

The statues represented: first Apollo (to whom the offering was dedicated – now lost) followed by Acnonius, a statesman, tetrarch of Thessaly and father of Agias, Telemachus and Agelaus. Then the pancratiast Agias and his two brothers – Telemachus (of whose statue nothing has been preserved) and Agelaus, the youngest of the three and a great runner. The family line continued with Daochus I, son of Agias and himself a tetrarch of Thessaly, with his son Sisyphus I, a military man, followed by his own son and dedicator of the offering Daochus II, whose statue has not been preserved. Last in the line was Sisyphus II, son of Daochus II. In the museum the statues are placed not in their original sequence but as demanded by the requirements of indoor space.

The first statue, then, – the naked young man standing apart – is Agias (Pl. 81), the grandfather of Daochus II and a famous champion at the pancratium (combined wrestling and boxing), many-times victor at panhellenic games – Olympic, Delphic, Isthmian and

Nemean – in the 5th century B.C. His image and that of his brother Agelaus are no por‑traits but idealised figures of athletes. They are believed to be marble copies of the earlier bronze originals that Daochus II had dedicated to Pharsala around 340 B.C. and were the work of the celebrated sculptor Lysippus of Sicyon, who specialised in bronze statuary, esp. of athletes, and was appointed sculptor to Alexander the Great.

In Agias – the best preserved of all the statues – one admires the easy posture in which the main masses of the body are in equilibrium. The athlete is shown at the moment when he has just overcome his adversary but, as shown by the eager expression on his powerful, energetic face, is ready, if need be, to start afresh with another opponent. He is wearing the victor's headdress around his head.

The next statue is Sisyphus II, son of the dedicator Daochus II; he is represented as a naked young man, his left elbow leaning on an archaic herma – the herma symbolising perhaps the supporting force this youngest member of the family drew from the greatness of his race.

The next statue is Agias's younger brother Agelaus, a race victor crowned at the Pythian Games. Agelaus lacks the fullgrown muscular strength of Agias who is shown in the prime of his manhood; his is rather the well-trained body of an adolescent with a lovely, pensive, face and strong, nervy legs.

Standing next to Agelaus is Sisyphus I, grandson of Agias, with a short, artfully worked chiton, his right hand raised in a sort of military commanding gesture, his cloak slung over his bent left arm (Pl. 82). His posture is not entirely frontal, there is a slight twist of the body. Thus, when seen on its pedestal, the statue would seem to turn towards the centre of the group. This work anticipates what later became a common type of Roman Emperor statue.

The next image is that of Acnonius, son of Aparus, first of his race and tetrarch of Thes‑saly, wearing a chlamys with folds so realistic, they seem to have movement in them. The posture indicates that as he was standing on his pedestal with Apollo on the one side and his descendants on the other, he made a broad, solemn gesture as if he were introducing the latter to the former.

The last statue is Daochus I, son of Agias, also a tetrarch of Thessaly, wrapped in unbend‑ing solemnity in a heavy chlamys with vertical folds on the left side.

An interesting point, if one considers that these statues stood all in a row on their lengthy base, is the artist's successful effort to avoid monotony by diversifying the postures, the move‑ments, the garments and the presentation of their folds.

The last exhibit in the room is a marble statue of an old man, a typical example of Greek portrayal art of the 3th century B.C., in which, apart from the skilful use of the chisel, an as yet timid utilization of the auger can be observed. It probably represents a philosopher or a priest and is an original work dating from 280–270 B.C. (Pl. 83).

XI. The Room of the Charioteer: The bronze statue in this room is one of the finest and most important original bronze plastic works of antiquity. It represents a charioteer, i.e. driver of a race chariot, in life-size (height 1.80 m.) at the moment when, his victorious race just over, he triumphantly presents his chariot to the applauding crowd (Pl. 62).

The Charioteer and the four-horse chariot (a quadriga) with a young groom holding the reins of the right-hand horse, constituted an impressive whole offered to Apollo by Poly‑zalus, tyrant of Gela (a Greek city in Sicily), son of Deinomenes and brother of Hieron, Gelon and Thrasybulos (see p. 19) in gratitude for his chariot-race victory at the Pythian Games in 478 or 474 B.C. The group was erected at the northwestern part of the sanctuary of Apollo, somewhere between the theatre and the wall known as *Ischegaon* (see p. 22) east of the recess of Crateros. The 373 B.C. earthquake which destroyed the temple and nearby buildings and monuments, hurled down the Charioteer and his chariot and covered them entirely with dirt and rocks.

The extensive French excavations of 1896 brought back to light the statue of the Charioteer, a part of its base with a fragment of the votive inscription, parts of the horses and the chariot, and a child's hand. With the exception of the left hand which has been lost, the statue is in very good condition, covered with the attractive green patina that has protected it from erosion.

An athletic youth with broad shoulders but delicate features, obviously of noble descent, a typical example of the young aristocracy of his time, the Charioteer is wearing the typical long chiton of the chariot-race competitors – the *xystis* – which reaches down to his delicate ankles in long parallel folds starting from the belt. The belt is placed high above the waist – which lends the statue an air of nimbleness. A view formerly held, that this position of the belt was deliberately chosen to create a disproportion, is no longer considered correct. The simple truth is that this is where the belt was normally worn with the customary attire of charioteers, and that the artist was merely being realistic. The chiton is fastened on the chest by means of two thin strips which pass under the armholes and cross high up at the back, thus preventing the garment from becoming inflated with air during the race.

The Charioteer's posture has a natural ease. His extended hands held the reins and his long, delicate fingers clutched, apart from the reins – a cylindrical object, the so-called *kentron* (a prick). The long and powerful neck supports a fine oval head which broadens at the level of the temples; the face wears an expression so intent, it takes the onlooker's breath away. The small ears are surrounded by locks in relief. The hair is tousled and clinging as if it were wet with the perspiration of the race. A broad band around the temples and the forehead – perfunctorily fastened at the back of the neck and decorated with a meander of impressed silver and bronze – marks the victor.

The chin is heavy and strong, the cheeks somewhat rounded, and the full, half-opened lips were probably coated with a thin foil of reddish bronze. The almond-shaped eyes are made of white enamel for the eyeball and brown stone for the iris, which is surrounded by a black circle and tightly encircles the round black spot of the pupil, thus lending the look a singular intensity.

The face is turned to the right and shows a slight asymmetry in the features, which makes it unusually expressive and alivelooking. The uncovered parts of the body – the hands and the feet – are executed with marvelous realism. One almost sees the life-blood throbbing through one vein at the bend of the arm and another at one foot. The body presents a slight twist which starts from the solidly treading feet and proceeds upwards through the hips, the shoulders, the head, and finally the glance. The austere geometrical style combines with gay naturalism and realism in the details to form a unique work of art that is human and idealistic, spiritual and eternal. The Charioteer, a contemporary of Aeschylus, Pindar and Bacchylides, the product of an era inspired with genuine religious faith, is the work of a great artist. Who this artist was is uncertain, but two likely hypotheses have been proposed: According to the one, the author of the Charioteer is Pythagoras of Samos, a renowned bronze-worker then in exile at Regium, Calabria. According to the second hypothesis, the Charioteer is the work of the Athenian sculptor Critias, known from his composition «Tyrant-Slayers», or at least of a disciple of Critias. Whatever the case may be, the statue is an example of the austere style of Attic art.

In the large showcase are kept the fragments of the horses of the Charioteer's chariot: two legs, a hoof, a tail and pieces of the reins.

At the far end of the room, on the right, there is a fragment of the base of the Charioteer, bearing remains of the votive inscription, which reads:

$[$-υῦ υῦ -υ $Π]$ολύζαλός μ' ἀνέθηκ[εν]
$[$-υῦ υῦ-]ον ἄεξ' εὐόνυμ' Ἀπολλ[ον]

The last exhibit in this room is a magnificently worked bronze censer (Pl. 63), an original work by some great artist, consisting of the figure of a young woman (16 cm. high), wearing the garment known as *peplos* and carrying on her head a small hemispherical container for the incense. Just visible under the long garment is the right footwear with upturned tip. Noteworthy is further the type of headdress known as *cecryphalos*, which entirely conceals the hair (460–450 B.C.).

XII. The Room of Antinoos: The Paros marble statue of a young man (130–138 A.D.) represents Antinoos from Claudiopolis of Bithynia (Pl. 60 - 61), celebrated for his beauty, and a companion of the Emperor of Rome Hadrian who was a well-known classicist and in the second century A.D., attempted to revive the Greek classical spirit in art and religion at the Greek cities and sanctuaries.

After his premature death (he drowned in the Nile), Antinoos was worshipped as a demi-god in all the cities and sanctuaries of the Greeks. Statues of him were erected everywhere and coins were made with his image. Through the intermediary of Titus Flavius Aristotimus (see p. 28), priest of Apollo, Delphi – having received many and varied favours from Hadrian – accorded high honours to Antinoos, including new coins and this statue which was erected in the great sanctuary behind the temple of Apollo. The statue is very well preserved and is considered one of the finest cult images of Antinoos and a representative sample of the art and spirit of the age.

The head, surrounded by rich locks of hair reaching down to the neck and cheeks and covering the ears, leaning to the left, was crowned with a thin wreath of gold laurel leaves. The gracefully rounded chin, the full lips, the dreamy eyes, combine to form an esthetically idealised face. This may be the moment when Antinoos has just crowned himself – a symbolic act signifying the ascent to higher-than human, divine spheres. The general attitude of the statue and in particular the inclinaton of the head seems to support this view.

Antinoos is a characteristic example of neoclassical art. Its polished surface which still maintains its shine (the ancients used to polish statues, especially cult images, with oil; they called this polishing *ganosis*) indicates that the statue had actually been an object of worship.

Across from Antinoos there is a headless herma-like pillar representing Plutarch, the writer who was also a priest of Apollo (50 – 125 A.D. approx.). It has been remarked that the epigram on this pillar – *Delphi and the citizens of Chaeronea offered this statue of Plutarch obeying the orders of the Amphictyonia* – «is a sad and somewhat jarring echo of the epigram of the dead of Thermopylae» *.

To the left of the pillar of Plutarch there is a statue representing a small boy carrying a goose (late 3rd century B.C.) and further on a fine Paros marble head dating from the second century B.C. (198–194 B.C.), probably representing the well-known Roman patrician, consul and proconsul Titus Quinctius Flamininus who, after defeating the king of Macedonia Philip V at the famous battle of Kynos Kephalae in 197 B.C., proclaimed one year later at the Isthmian Games the liberty of Greece and the independence of the Greek cities. He was therefore honoured as a liberator by many Greek cities, many statues of him were erected and even new games were instituted in his honour. In addition to this head, a base was found at Delphi which, according to the inscription engraved on it, supported a bronze statue of this noble Roman.

The head represents him at a young age, around 30, when he was a consul. The round head, the hair covering the neck and the forehead in deliberate unconcern, the short beard, the narrow nose, the noble forehead furrowed by two wrinkles, the low eyebrows, the full cheeks, the ironic smile, the wilful chin, all contribute to the making of a unique portrait.

---

* CHR. KAROUSOS

The unknown artist, who was undoubtedly gifted with great psychological insight, and perhaps drew inspiration from the Attic tradition in the art of portrayal, has succeeded in masterfully expressing the manifold personality of the young Roman aristocrat – his intense psychic activity compounded of wisdom and vanity, will-power and ambition (Pl. 63).

The marble statue of the smiling little girl is a commonplace work of the early 3rd century B.C. (Pl. 84).

The last sculptural work in the room is another portrait made of Paros marble (Pl. 85), part of a herma, wearing a gentle and thoughtful expression, and features revealing intense preoccupation with spiritual matters. It represents an unknown philosopher of the period of the Emperors (2nd century A.D.).

To complete the description of the museum, it is necessary to refer briefly to the contents of the showcases in this room. The ones standing against the walls contain pottery, figurines and jewellery from Delphi and the surrounding area.

The first showcase, the one nearest to the statue of Antinoos, exhibits in the middle part of the lower shelf: vases of the early Helladic period (2500–2000 B.C. approximately), vases etc. of the late Helladic period (Mycenaean I and II) (1600–1400 B.C. approx.) in the middle part of the upper shelf and pottery of the middle Helladic period (2000–1600 B.C. approx.) in the other parts. This pottery was found during excavations at the sites of the cities of Krissa and Cirrha, then rivals of Delphi.

The second showcase contains vases of the late Helladic (Mycenaean III) period (1400–1100 B.C. approx.) from the city and the graveyards of Delphi (the two vessels at the right-hand extremity of the lower shelf were found in a tomb at Itea. Most of the figurines were found at the sanctuary of Athene Pronaia (see p. 4 and 26).

The third showcase includes vases of the so-called Geometric period (– 8th century B.C.), from Delphi. Note that the vessels displayed on the upper shelf were found all together when a house of that period was uncovered.

The fourth showcase contains early Corinthian pottery (late 8th century to middle 7th century B.C.), found during excavations of ancient houses at Delphi (lower shelf and left part of middle shelf), and in tombs at Amfissa (middle and right-hand part of middle shelf), as well as jewellery and pottery of the Post-Geometric period (which is closely connected with the early Corinthian): brooches, bracelets, a clasp, hairpins (upper shelf).

The fifth showcase, the one at the short wall of the room contains clay pottery and figurines found at a sanctuary of Cirrha, the port of Krissa. These objects cover a long period of time, from the destruction of Cirrha in 590 B.C. down to the period of activity of the Athenian orator Aeschines in 339–338 B.C. The objects displayed in the showcase represent only a small part of the total number found and present remarkable diversity: they include Corinthian pottery of the 5th century, Attic pottery of the 5th century the closed kylix of the austere style period is a particularly fine sample; on its upper surface can be seen the remains of a symposium scene while the lower surface is ornamented with Dionysiac scenes; pottery of the 4th century – tiny vase offerings, a great variety of figurines from the 6th, 5th and 4th centuries (standing and seated deities, female masks), a rather large slab with a relief showing a sitting goddess, animal figurines (pigs, turtles, birds), small slabs with representations of wasps and flying Gorgons, oil-lamps (one is multiple), and finally a bronze statuette of a roe.

Coming now to the showcases in the middle of the room: the first (behind the pillar of Plutarch) contains objects found during the excavation of the Corycian Cave, a spacious cave on Mt. Parnassus, sacred to Pan and the Nymphs. Though these findings are by no means impressive – most were humble offerings by poor mountaineers – yet they give a fairly clear idea of what this type of cult caves were like. Pilgrims to them usually offered things of small value – clay figurines of gods, men, animals, astragals (some of them in bronze), small, insignificant vessels; occasionally, there were offerings of relatively higher value, such as the black-figure slab showing satyrs and nymphs, the plate representing the quarrel between Hercules and Apollo about the Delphic tripod, rings (some of silver with figures).

The second showcase includes bronze objects and statuettes of the Geometric period (8th century to early 7th century B.C.): on the upper shelf, statuettes of men, on the middle shelf images of animals, on the lower shelf legs and handles of tripods (Pl. 64). Note the upper part of one tripod leg presenting a winged goddess.

Bronze griffin from the decoration of a cauldron.

The third showcase includes mainly parts of bronze tripods and cauldrons of the 8th and 7th century B.C. On the upper shelf, griffins which served as cauldron decorations (Pl. 64), on the middle shelf, bull heads and covers with a human head, feathers and tail of a bird (importations from the Orient and Greek imitations, 8th - 7th century B.C.); on the lower shelf animal heads, a tripod leg with a Cypriot inscription, lionesses and other animals.

The fourth showcase contains statuettes of men and animals for the most part. A remarkable exhibit on the upper shelf is the statuette of a young man with outstretched arms (perhaps Apollo claiming the prophetic tripod from Hercules - see p. 36) dating from approximately 470 B.C., the statuette of a flute-player (approx. 500 B.C. Pl. 64) and a statuette of the early Hellenistic period – Dionysus or Apollo. On the middle shelf there is a fine statuette of a youth wearing a jacket (last quarter of 5th century B.C.) from the Spercheios plain. Interesting are also the two sphinxes facing each other on Ionic capitals, as well as the plinths with feet of men, the wild bird, the small cover representing a ram and Ulysses tied beneath it (Pl. 64) – a representation of the well-known episode at the cave of Polyphemus – and two other cover decorations: Eurystheus in the jar and Hercules with the boar on his shoulders. On the lower shelf, there are statuettes of animals (the two dog heads are from the decoration of a bed).

The fifth showcase contains mainly bronze vessels and decorative elements of such vessels. On the upper shelf, vertical handles of water and wine pitchers are shown, with a human head as an emblem at the lower end. Noteworthy is the handle consisting of a charging lion (second half of 6th century B.C.) and, for its shape, the half perfume-flask in the form of a turtle. On the middle shelf are some miniature vessels – three flasks (the one, which is Phoenician and dates from the 8th century B.C., represents a siege), an oil-lamp shaped like a funny face (Hellenistic period), animals, etc. On the lower shell are displayed circular vase bases with three lion legs (Archaic period), basin handles in the form of open flowers (7th cent. B.C.), a handle from the cover of a utensil in the shape of two dolphins (Roman period) and a plastic representation of the bolt of lightning of Zeus.

The sixth showcase exhibits weapons and a few objects of feminine beauty care. On the upper shelf there are helmets of the 7th and 6th century B.C. The one with two seams is of the Illyric type, the others are Corinthian. One is decorated with an anthemion in relief, another with an engraved representation of a rooster between two lions. On the middle shelf are displayed copper strips with reliefs; these were sewn on leather strips and put inside shields (6th century B.C.), two mirrors – one of them quite plain with an inscription ARCHIPPA

ELYTHIA, the other with a female head in relief (Classical period), clasps (8th century B.C.), bracelets and brooches (7th century B.C.). On the lower shelf there are axes, a sword in its sheath (from a bronze statue), arrow tips (some unfinished), javelin tips, a weight inscribed HIERA MM (= sacred mna) i.e. a double-mna dedicated to Apollo.

Looking out from the windows of the vestibule of the museum, one can see (in front of the museum) a fine mosaic which was the floor of an early Christian basilica of the 5th century A.D., found in 1959 in the present village of Delphi. The brightness of the colours and the vividness of the human and animal figures is worthy of note.

In the part of the mosaic which is near the sarcophagus, there are birds enclosed in circles, while in the middle part, the central representation of a panther devouring a deer is surrounded by peacocks, eagles, and two young men carrying baskets of fruit (Pl. 86). The rest of the mosaic consists of animal figures: a camel, a goat, a donkey, a cat with a mouse in its mouth, a dog, a lion, a deer, a hen, a wild boar, etc., and in-between the animals there are fish and other sea creatures.

The sarcophagus near the mosaic is an ordinary work without artistic value. It was uncovered in the so-called eastern graveyard of ancient Delphi (east of the sanctuary of Athene Pronaia) and is decorated with reliefs: the hunt of Meleager and two griffins facing each other on either side of a torch. On the cover of the sarcophagus, there is the lying figure of the dead person.

It only remains to refer briefly to the roofed space in front of the museum. Displayed there are some of the innumerable inscriptions of Delphi, most of them dedications; architectural members of buildings and monuments found in the sanctuary of Apollo; and one female statue. These exhibits, though very important in some aspects, present no general interest.

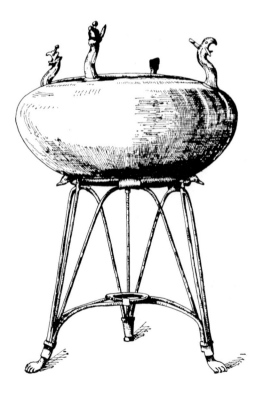

Ἐρείπια ρωμαϊκῆς ἀγορᾶς.
Ruines de l'agora romaine.
Ruins of Roman agora (marketplace).
Ruinen des römischen Marktes.

Τὰ ἐρείπια τοῦ θησαυροῦ τῶν Σικυωνίων.
Les ruines du trésor des Sicyoniens.
The ruins of the treasury of Sicyon.
Ruinen des Schatzhauses der Sikyonier.

Ὁ θησαυρὸς τῶν Ἀθηναίων.
Le trésor des Athéniens.
The treasury of the Athenians.
Das Schatzhaus der Athener.

Ὁ μεγάλος πολυγωνικὸς τοῖχος τοῦ ἱεροῦ τοῦ Ἀπόλλωνος καὶ ἡ στοὰ τῶν Ἀθηναίων.
Le mur polygonal du sanctuaire d'Apollon et le portique des Athéniens.
The large polygonal wall of the sanctuary of Apollo and the Stoa of the Athenians.
Die große polygonale Stützmauer des Apollonheiligtumes und die Halle der Athener.

Ἡ ἱερὰ ὁδός. Ἀριστερὰ ἡ βάση τοῦ τρίποδα τῶν Πλαταιῶν.
La voie sacrée. À gauche la base du trépied de Platées.
The Sacred Way. On the left, the pedestal of the Tripod of Plataea.
Die heilige Straße. Links die Basis des Dreifußes von Plataiai.

Τὸ βάθρο τοῦ ἀγάλματος τοῦ βασιλιᾶ Προυσία.
Pilier de la statue équestre du roi Prusias.
The pedestal of the statue of King Prusias.
Der Sockel für die Statue Königs Prusias.

Ἄποψη τοῦ ναοῦ τοῦ Ἀπόλλωνος ἀπὸ Δυσμῶν.
Le temple d'Apollon vu de l'Ouest.
The temple of Apollo from the West.
Ansicht des Apollontempels vom Westen.

Ὁ ναὸς τοῦ Ἀπόλλωνος. Ἐμπρὸς ὁ βωμὸς τῶν Χίων.
Le temple d'Apollon. Devant le temple l'autel de Chios.
The temple of Apollo. In front, the altar of the Chians.
Der Apollontempel. Vor ihm der Altar der Chier.

Τὸ θέατρο τῶν Δελφῶν.
Le théâtre de Delphes.
The Theatre of Delphi.
Das Theater von Delphi.

Τὸ στάδιο τῶν Δελφῶν.
Le stade de Delphes.
The Stadium of Delphi.
Das Stadion von Delphi.

Ἡ πηγὴ Κασταλία.
La fontaine Castalie.
The Castalia fountain.
Die Quelle Kastaliά.

Γενικὴ ἄποψη τοῦ ἱεροῦ τοῦ Ἀπόλλωνος.
Vue générale du sanctuaire d'Apollon.

General view of the sanctuary of Apollo.
Allgemeine Ansicht des Apollonheiligtumes.

Ἡ Θόλος τοῦ ἱεροῦ τῆς Ἀθηνᾶς Προναίας.
La Tholos du sanctuaire d'Athéna Pronaia.
The Tholos of the sanctuary of Athene Pronaia.
Die Tholos (Rundbau) des Heiligtumes der Athena Pronaia.

Ὁ θριγκὸς τῆς Θόλου.
Entablement de la Tholos.
The entablature of the Tholos.
Das Gebälk der Tholos.

ες ποὺ χορεύουν ἐ-
ω σὲ κίονα.

ιes filles dansant sur
colonne végétale.

cing girls on col-
ι.

einer Säule tanzende
en.

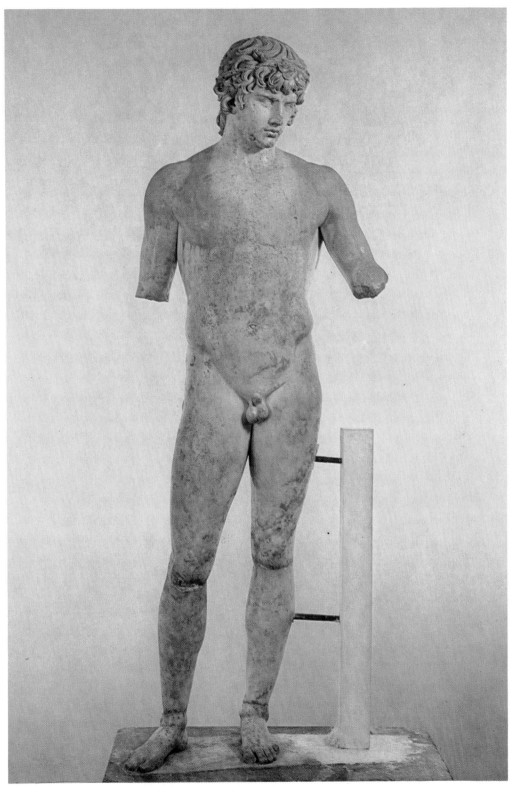

Ὁ Ἀντίνοος.   Antinoos.
Antinoüs.   Antinoos.

Τὸ χάλκινο ἄγαλμα τοῦ ἡνιόχου.
La statue en bronze de l'Aurige.
The Bronze statue of the Charioteer.
Die Bronzestatue des Wagenlenkers.

Χάλκινο θυμιατήριο.
Brûle-parfum en bronze.
Bronze censer.
Bronzenes Weihrauchgefäß.

'Ανδρική εἰκονιστική κεφαλή.
Portrait d'homme.
Head of a man.
Männlicher Porträtkopf.

Χάλκινη κεφαλὴ γρύπα.
Tête de griffon en bronze.
Bronze griffin head.
Bronzekopf eines Greifen.

Χάλκινο ἀγαλμάτιο αὐλητῆ.
Statuette en bronze d'un joueur de flûte.
Bronze statuette of a flute-player.
Bronzestatuette eines Flötenspielers

Ὁ Ὀδυσσεὺς κάτω ἀπὸ τὸν κριό.
Ulysse sous le bélier.
Ulysses under the ram.
Odysseus unter dem Bauch des Widers.

Λαβὴ χάλκινου τρίποδα.
Anse de trépied en bronze.
Handle of a bronze tripod.
Griff eines Bronzedreifußes.

Χάλκινο ἀγαλμάτιο νέου.
Statuette en bronze d'un jeune homme.
Bronze statuette of a youth.
Bronzestatuette eines Jünglings.

Χάλκινο ἀγαλμάτιο Ἀπόλλωνος.
Statuette d'Apollon en bronze.
Bronze statuette of Apollo.
Bronzestatuette Apollons.

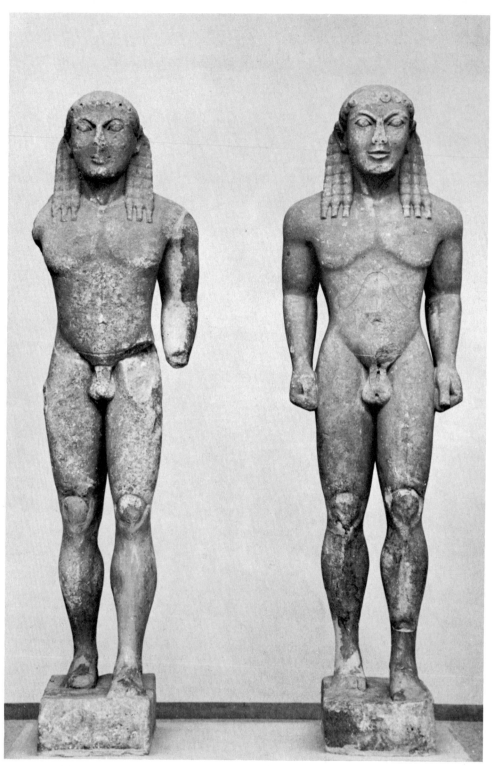

Δυὸ ἀρχαϊκὰ ἀγάλματα: ὁ Κλέοβις καὶ ὁ Βίτων.
Statues archaïques de Cléobis et Biton.
Two archaic statues: Cleovis and Biton.
Zwei archaische Statuen: Kleobis und Biton.

Μετόπη τοῦ μονοπτέρου τῆς Σικυῶνος: ὁ Καλυδώνιος Κάπρος.
Métope du monoptère sicyonien: le sanglier de Calydon.
Metope of the monopteros treasury of Sicyon: the Calydonian Boar.
Metope aus dem monopterus Schatzhaus der Sikyonier: Der Kalydonische Eber.

Τὸ ἀνατολικὸ ἀέτωμα τοῦ θησαυροῦ τῶν Σιφνίων.
Fronton Est du trésor de Siphnos.
The eastern pediment of the treasury of Siphnos.
Der Ostgiebel des Schatzhauses der Siphnier.

Θησαυρὸς Σιφνίων: ὁ Ἄρης, ἡ Ἀφροδίτη, ἡ Ἄρτεμις, ὁ Ἀπόλλων καὶ ὁ Ζεύς.
Trésor de Siphnos: Arès, Aphrodite, Artémis, Apollon et Zeus.
From the treasury of Siphnos: Ares (Mars), Aphrodite, Artemis, Apollo and Zeus.
Das Schatzhaus der Siphnier: Ares, Aphrodite, Artemis, Apollon und Zeus.

Θησαυρὸς Σιφνίων: ἡ Ἀθηνᾶ, ἡ Ἥρα καὶ ἡ Δήμητρα.
Trésor de Siphnos: Athéna, Héra et Déméter.
From the treasury of Siphnos: Athene, Hera and Demeter.
Das Schatzhaus der Siphnier: Athena, Hera und Demeter.

Θησαυρὸς Σιφνίων: ἅρμα τρωϊκὸ μὲ τὸν ἱπποκόμο του.
Trésor de Siphnos: char troyen avec son écuyer.
From the treasury of Siphnos: Trojan chariot with groom.
Das Schatzhaus der Siphnier: Trojanisches Viergespann mit seinem Wagenlenker.

Θησαυρὸς Σιφνίων: μάχη ἐμπρὸς ἀπὸ τὴν Τροία. Ὁ Αἰνείας, ὁ Ἕκτωρ, νεκρὸς πολεμιστής, ὁ
Μενέλαος καὶ ὁ Αἴας.
Trésor de Siphnos: bataille devant Troie. Énée, Hector, guerrier mort, Ménélas et Ajax.
From the treasury of Siphnos: Battle outside Troy: Aeneias, Hector, dead warrior, Menelaus
and Ajax.
Das Schatzhaus der Siphnier: Schlacht vor Troja: Aeneas, Hektor, toter Krieger, Menelaos
und Ajax.

Θησαυρὸς Σιφνίων: ὁ Ἀπόλλων, ἡ Ἄρτεμις, γίγας σὲ φυγή, τρεῖς γίγαντες.
Trésor de Siphnos: Apollon, Artémis, géant en fuite, trois géants.
From the treasury of Siphnos: Apollo, Artemis, a fleeing giant, three giants.
Das Schatzhaus der Siphnier: Apollon, Artemis, flüchtender Gigant, drei Giganten.

Θησαυρὸς Σιφνίων: ὁ Ἄρης, ὁ γίγας Ἀστάρτας νεκρός, οἱ γίγαντες Βιάτας καὶ Ἐνάφας.
Trésor de Siphnos: Arès, le géant Astartas mort, les géants Biatas et Enaphas.
From the treasury of Siphnos: Ares, the giant Astartas dead, the giants Biatas and Enaphas.
Das Schatzhaus der Siphnier: Ares, der tote Gigant Astartas, die Giganten Biatas und Enaphas.

Θησαυρὸς Σιφνίων: ἡ ᾿Αφροδίτη κατεβαίνει ἀπὸ τὸ ἅρμα της.
Trésor de Siphnos: Aphrodite descendant de son char.
From the treasury of Siphnos: Aphrodite stepping off her chariot.
Das Schatzhaus der Siphnier: die ihrem Wagen entsteigende Aphrodite.

Θησαυρὸς Σιφνίων: τέθριππο ἐμπρὸς σὲ βωμό.
Trésor de Siphnos: quadrige devant un autel.
From the treasury of Siphnos: Four-horse chariot (quadriga) in front of an altar.
Das Schatzhaus der Siphnier: Viergespann vor einem Altar.

71

Καρυᾶτις τοῦ θησαυροῦ τῶν Σιφνίων.
Caryatide du trésor de Siphnos.
Caryatid from the treasury of Siphnos.
Karyatide des Schatzhauses der Siphnier.

Κεφαλὴ Καρυάτιδος.
Tête de Caryatide.
Head of Caryatid.
Kopf einer Karyatide.

Ἡ σφίγγα τῶν Ναξίων.
Le sphinx des Naxiens.
The sphinx of Naxos.
Die Sphinx der Naxier.

Μετόπη τοῦ θησαυροῦ τῶν Ἀθηναίων: ὁ
Θησεὺς καὶ ἡ Ἀντιόπη.
Métope du trésor des Athéniens: Thé-
sée et Antiope.
Metope from the treasury of the Athe-
nians: Theseus and Antiope.
Metope aus dem Schatzhaus der Athe-
ner: Theseus und Antiope.

Μετόπη τοῦ θησαυροῦ τῶν Ἀθηναίων: ὁ
Ἡρακλῆς καὶ ὁ Κύκνος.
Métope du trésor des Athéniens: Héra-
clès et Kycnos.
Metope from the treasury of the Athe-
nians: Hercules and Cycnus.
Metope aus dem Schatzhaus der Athe-
ner: Herakles und Kyknos.

Μετόπη τοῦ θησαυροῦ τῶν Ἀθηναίων: ὁ Ἡρακλῆς καὶ ἡ Κερυνῖτις ἔλαφος.
Métope du trésor des Athéniens: Héraclès et le cerf aux pieds d'airain.
Metope from the treasury of the Athenians: Hercules and the Ceryneian Hind.
Metope aus dem Schatzhaus der Athener: Herakles und der Kerynetische Hirsch.

Τὸ ἀνατολικὸ ἀέτωμα τοῦ ἀρχαϊκοῦ ναοῦ τοῦ Ἀπόλλωνος.
Fronton Est du temple archaïque d'Apollon.
The eastern pediment of the archaic temple of Apollo.
Der Ostgiebel des archaischen Apollontempels.

Νίκη φτερωτή, ἀκρωτήριο τοῦ ναοῦ τοῦ Ἀπόλλωνος.
Niké (Victoire ailée), acrotère du temple archaïque d'Apollon.
Winged Victory, an acroterium from the temple of Apollo.
Geflügelte Nike. Akroter des Apollontempels.

Τμῆμα ὑδρορρόης τοῦ ναοῦ τοῦ Ἀπόλλωνος τοῦ 4ου αἰ. π.Χ.
Chéneau du temple d'Apollon du IVe s. av. J.-C.
A part of the drain - pipe of the 4th-century - B.C. temple of Apollo.
Simafragment des Apollontempels aus dem 4. Jahrhundert v. Chr.

Ἐπιτύμβια στήλη νέου.
Stèle funéraire d'un jeune athlète.
Funerary stele of young man.
Grabstele eines Jünglings.

Κεφαλὴ ἀγάλματος τοῦ Διονύσου.
Tête de Dionysos.
Head of a statue of Dionysus.
Kopf einer Dionysosstatue.

Βωμὸς ἀπὸ τὸ ἱερὸ τῆς ᾿Αθηνᾶς Προναίας.
Autel provenant du sanctuaire d'Athéna Pronaia.
Altar from the sanctuary of Athene Pronaia.
Altar aus dem Heiligtum der Athena Pronaia.

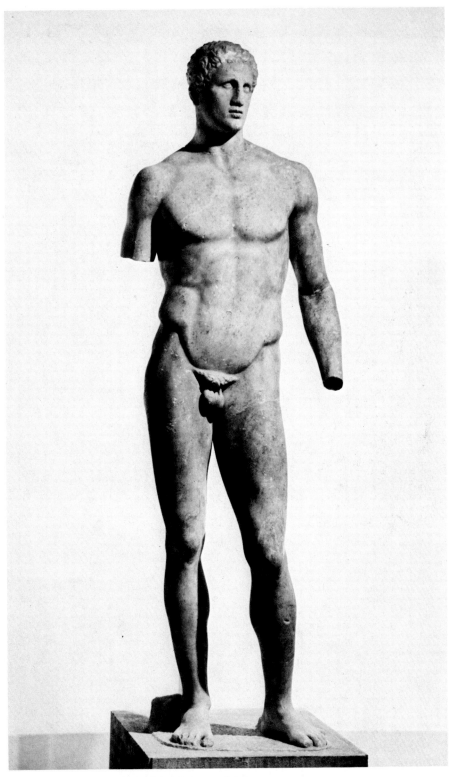

Τὸ ἄγαλμα τοῦ ἀθλητῆ Ἀγίου, ἀπὸ τὸ ἀφιέρωμα τοῦ Δαόχου.
Statue de l'athlète Agias: ex-voto de Daochos.
The statue of the athlete Agias, from the offering of Daochus.
Die Statue des Athleten Agias. Aus dem Daochosweihgeschenk.

Ὁ Σίσυφος Α΄, ἀπὸ τὸ ἀφιέρωμα τοῦ Δαόχου.
Statue de Sisyphos Iᵉʳ: ex-voto de Daochos.
Sisyphus I, from the offering of Daochus
Sisyphos I. Aus dem Daochosweihgeschenk.

Ἄγαλμα φιλοσόφου ἢ ἱερέα.
Statue d'un philosophe ou d'un prêtre.
Statue of a philosopher or priest.
Statue eines Philosophen oder eines Priesters.

Μαρμάρινο ἄγαλμα μικροῦ κοριτσιοῦ.
Statue d'une fillette souriant.
Marble statue of a girl child.
Marmorstatue eines kleinen Mädchens.

Μαρμάρινη κεφαλὴ φιλοσόφου.
Buste d'un philosophe.
Marble head of a philosopher.
Marmorkopf eines Philosophen.

Ψηφιδωτή παράσταση νέου πού κρατάει κάνιστρο.
Jeune homme en mosaïque portant une corbeille.
Mosaic representing a youth holding a basket.
Mosaikdarstellung eines Jünglings mit einem Korb.

«ΟΙ ΔΕΛΦΟΙ»
ΤΟΥ
ΒΑΣΙΛΕΙΟΥ ΠΕΤΡΑΚΟΥ
ΤΥΠΩΘΗΚΑΝ
ΣΤΟ ΕΡΓΟΣΤΑΣΙΟ
ΓΡΑΦΙΚΩΝ ΤΕΧΝΩΝ
Ι. ΜΑΚΡΗ Α.Ε.
ΓΙΑ ΛΟΓΑΡΙΑΣΜΟ
ΤΗΣ ΕΚΔΟΤΙΚΗΣ
ΕΠΙΧΕΙΡΗΣΕΩΣ
Σ. Ι. ΒΙΓΛΑ & ΣΙΑ
ΕΚΔΟΣΕΙΣ «ΕΣΠΕΡΟΣ»